To: Lukas,

Live and Enjoy the blessings from your Amazing life.

Gerald L. Hunt
4/17 2015

I AM AMAZED!

You are truly special. Stay strong!!

I Am Amazed!

Reflections on an Awe-Inspired Life

By

Gerald L. Durley

With Ben Campbell Johnson

Pathways Press
Atlanta, Georgia

ISBN-13:
978-1-5005-6476-6

ISBN-10:
1-500-56476-1

Copies of this book may be ordered from:
www.Amazon.com
in both print and Kindle editions

or from:
Pathways Press
PO Box 98213
Atlanta GA 30359

Contents

Preface

A FEW MONTHS AGO, I retired from a congregation where I had been the pastor for twenty-five years. Being retired offers its own challenges, but I am confident that life does not end with retirement. As long as I am alive, there is a calling on my life, a compelling to do something that will make a difference in the world. One of the first things I decided to do was to reflect on my seventy years of life – where I was born, how I grew up and what I have done with these years I've had. Somehow I believe that the fruit of the future will be drawn from the roots of my past. Remembering and recording all those things that have made me who I am today was a sobering and rewarding experience. In the years of my life, I have been through times of poverty and plenty, through being settled and uprooted and through periods of struggle and overflowing fulfillment.

I began this reflection by going back as far as I could remember and recalling those persons, experiences and influences that have shaped who I, Gerald L. Durley, truly am. I realized, as never before, the impact that my grandmother had on me as a child – she taught me so much about how to live in the world. As I reviewed my life, I bumped into the influence of my mother and father, my grade school teachers, my high school and college basketball coaches, the deans of my various universities, the early leaders of the Civil Rights Movement, and also those persons who trusted me and increasingly gave me new responsibilities.

In addition to these influential persons, there is a host of men and women who have taught me much about ministry in the world. They would include Dr. C. T. Vivian, Dr. Joseph Roberts, Ambassador Andrew Young, Dr. Samuel Dewitt Proctor, Dr. Marvin Powell, Dr. Rhoten Smith, Dr. Frank Harrington, Dr. Don Bigelow, Dr. Wilton Anderson, Dr. Elias Blake, Dr. Frederick S. Humphries, Dr. Lawrence Neil Jones, Bill Siphax, Dr. Aaron B. Mackley, Dr. Benjamin Elijah Mays, Dr. Billy Graham, Rev. Dan Southern, Mayors Maynard H. Jackson, Shirley Franklin, Bill Campbell, Kasim Reed, Governor Roy Barnes, President Barack Obama, Attorney Michael Tyler and Banker George Andrews. I was reluctant to share these memories, but my friend Ben Johnson saw something in me that I did not see. He not only encouraged me to share these reflections, but he was a resource in writing this text. I will forever be indebted and grateful to him and to his brilliant wife, Nan, whom I got to know during the writing of this story. Of course, I alone am fully responsible for any errors or omissions.

Writing these personal reflections has caused me to feel a deeper affection for my daughter, Nia, and my son, Hasan, and his wife Kenya. These two remarkable children have been a source of strength as I have given much of my time, energy and financial resources to so many others. Neither of our children has ever been in any serious trouble nor have they abandoned the faith. They are role models for young people and proof that good people do not finish last. Both of our children and our daughter-in-law have been a source of great fulfillment in our lives. After the illness that affected our family, we have, on a regular basis, spent more time together building our family and enjoying life. My daughter Nia has been a lifelong blessing. Her children, Tai and Tori, have been a source of joy for Muriel and me. Hasan's and Kenya's children, Niara and Jelani, are also a spiritual blessing to us.

My expression of my feelings for all these friends and other members of my family have not included the one person who has meant more to me than all others combined, my wife, Muriel. Muriel, these memories are all laced with your smile, your steady hand and the manner in which you have fulfilled my life completely. Thank you for sharing this life with me.

If the past is a prelude to the future, I believe that life on earth and beyond holds a joy and delight that I cannot even imagine. I am dedicating the remainder of my life to helping people come alive again to the fullness and joy that is ours as we live and serve. Will you join me in this great effort to help people come alive here and now?

- Gerald L. Durley

Dedicated to my loving wife, Muriel,
my children, Nia and Hasan,
my grandchildren Tai, Tori, Niara, and Jelani;
Mama and Daddy, Grandma,
Rev. Dr. George B. Wirth,
Rev. Timothy McDonald
and countless others
-- YOU KNOW WHO YOU ARE --
who have made my life's journey so AMAZING!!

CHAPTER ONE

✪

A Litany of Amazement

I AM AMAZED! My eyes have been opened, my ears have been unplugged, my heart is made to quiver as I look back reviewing the life I have been given.

I am amazed, utterly and completely blown away, by the constant goodness of God in my one and only life.

I am amazed that a Black baby boy born to a sixteen-year-old girl in a poor neighborhood in Kansas could rise to be a friend and confidant of mayors, governors, presidents and faith leaders around the world.

I am amazed that an industrious father, a preacher of the gospel, took our small family to California to give his son a chance to grow up in an area without the visible prejudice against Black people that existed in other parts of the country.

I am amazed that this boy grew to be a six-foot-five giant of a man, who could leap high enough to stuff a basketball through the hoop.

I am amazed at the wisdom implanted in this child by a loving, snuff-dipping grandmother who never ceased to love her grandson no matter what happened.

I am amazed that the Providence of God drew this tall young man to Tennessee State University in Nashville, Tennessee, when he had scholarship offers from numerous top universities.

I am amazed that a young man who grew up in poor surroundings could enter the university, get an education and graduate without owing one copper cent.

I am amazed that God sent into this life the right person, at the right time, and in the right place to create opportunity, wholeness and recognition that made him who he is today.

I am amazed that a big, strong, Black man could endure prejudice, rejection and insults simply because his skin was Black and that he could control himself when the stones of criticism were cast his way.

I am amazed that this man had the courage to join the Civil Rights Movement, follow Dr. Martin Luther King, Jr. and seek to make a difference in the world at a time when it was an unpopular thing to do.

Is this too much amazement for you, dear reader?

This litany of amazement is just beginning. . . .

I am amazed that a jobless man sheltered from the world had an opportunity to travel the world, meet important people and make enough money to provide for a wife and two children.

I am amazed that a man who was filled with curiosity, drinking wine, playing sports and just having fun in Africa, never got to Paris, but landed in Neuchâtel, Switzerland, where he met the woman who was to complement his life and support him in all that he attempted.

I am amazed that a man who served his country in the Peace Corps, one who had an above average GPA, got rejections from numerous universities across America, even though his college grades and Peace Corps service were impeccable.

I am amazed that the same university that gave him a chance to earn a master's degree, made him a counselor and trusted him to be responsible for recruiting high school graduates to join "CHANCE," an African-American studies program .

I am amazed that the man in charge of a program in the United States Office of Education would call this university administrator to take a job directing the Career Opportunities Program and would move him and his wife to Washington D, C.

I am amazed that a struggling kid raised in the cotton fields of Bakersfield, California, would rise to a position from which he led professors and administrators from Black colleges across America.

I am amazed that an unexpected baby, whose mother never completed high school, earned a Ph.D. from the University of Massachusetts.

I am amazed that a first grader who could not speak without stuttering and was judged to be retarded, grew into a man who would speak to national gatherings of educators, labor unions, religious devotees, political constituents and social workers without difficulty.

I am amazed that at a time when this man was in turmoil and confusion, doors opened, words of encouragement came and courage arose to make choices that not only changed his life, but changed his world more than he could have ever dreamed.

I am amazed that God answered prayer when his son lay at death's door and was returned to him, and the boy's mother, healthy and whole.

I am amazed that in the hours of grief and fear, this man turned toward heaven and promised to do whatever God wanted him to do, if only God would save his son, a promise that took him in directions he never would have imagined.

I am amazed that a man who had rejected religion wound up going to seminary and studying the Bible and theology; and I am unbelievably shocked that he became a minister of a Missionary Baptist Church.

I am amazed that a man who was deeply dedicated to the Civil Rights Movement was late for the departure of the Freedom Riders bus and escaped being beaten and harassed when those who were on the bus were stopped in Alabama, then beaten and arrested while the bus was burned.

I am amazed that a little church of 200 members could grow and grow and grow until it reached over 1,500 members, who were alive to God and actively engaged in transforming their community into a just and loving society.

I am amazed that a church that traditionally had only one minister expanded and ordained over a hundred lay members to empower the larger membership to engage in the mission to our community: providing food and clothing for families, resisting injustice in the jails, educating adults and children alike, engaging in the formation of children and youth, responding to scores of other needs.

I am amazed and humbled at all the awards that have been given to this man who never intended to become a preacher:

Lifetime Building Bridges Achievement Award (The Atlanta Islamic Speakers Bureau)
Inducted into the Civil Rights Walk of Fame
Recipient of the Black Student Engineers Achievement Award
Peace and Environmental Award (Arava Institute)
National Award from North American Association for Environmental Educators
Atlanta's Fire Station #25 (Recognition)
American Medical Association Honoree
The Chozen Award
Billy Graham Crusade Co-Chair
Journal of Famous Speeches (Inclusion)
Fulton County Red Cross Partner
The Beltline Highway Commission Board Member
The Celebration of Achievements Award Honoree
Morehouse Medical School Annual Achievement Award
"Keepers of the Dream" Award
African Heritage Award
Association of Black Social Workers – Harambee Award
Atlanta Department of Parks, Recreation and Cultural Affairs – Teen Week Award

I am amazed at all the speeches, addresses and invocations that this preacher gave during his twenty-five years of pastoral work:

Invocation at City Hall
Speech at "Rally to Success"
Invocation at The Freedom Center on its 38th Anniversary
A keynote address on Founder's Day at the Freedom Center
Invocation at the State Capital of Georgia honoring Martin Luther King, Jr. and Hosea Williams
Speech on racism at Presbytery of Greater Atlanta

Speech at Emory Health Ministries Association
Speech at the South Carolina Conference on Aging
Special presentation at a James Weldon Johnson
    commemoration at Emory University – A Remembrance of
    God's Trombones
Address to The National Conference on Crime Victims' Rights
Commencement address at Tennessee State University
Black Brother's Day speech
Speech to National Association of Black Social Workers

CHAPTER TWO

✪

I Am Amazed at the Formation of My Life

THE AMAZEMENT OF MY LIFE cannot be seen clearly unless we look through the lenses of my earliest years. If you only know about the preacher Gerald Durley, then you know very little of the man. You would first have to know the influences that shaped him and the lessons of life that made him. To begin to understand me, you must know that I was born in 1942 on the plains of Wichita, Kansas, into the home of a poor Black family. When I was born, my mother was sixteen and my father was nineteen. In my early years, I spent lots of time with my grandmother, who taught me many things about life.

My father worked at the Boeing airplane factory in Wichita during the day and played music in various musical establishments at night. He played the trumpet and piano in a small, put together band. My father had a high school education and struggled to make enough money to feed himself, my mother and me. Not having much formal education beyond high school made it difficult for my mother to get a job and help earn a living. She was raised alongside two sisters in a single parent home. My mother was raised strictly by my grandmother, who placed very clear rules and demands on her daughters. My mother was a very quiet and reserved woman; she was also slim with distinct facial lines that made her stand out in a group. She and my father met in high school, and she was only fifteen years old when she fell in love with him.

My father, on the other hand, was from a musical family, and his whole family was somewhat boisterous. My grandmother on my father's side was known to be argumentative, which meant there was a great deal of banter back and forth in their family. My father was first a trumpet player, then a piano player. He was always industrious and was constantly seeking new adventures and new things to experience in life.

My mother was a responsible person until the day she died. One of my aunts shared a story with me about my mother and father coming to Wichita, Kansas for a visit. She told me that my mother packed all of her three children's clothes in one suitcase. My aunt said that she never felt more compassion for another person than she did for my mother, who was burdened with the responsibility of three small children. My father was constantly moving about; he always seemed to be busy and could not be in one place for too long. My mother was just the opposite; she also had an ability to control things with just a look. When any of us children did something wrong, she'd get an expression on her face that meant for us to change our behavior immediately. The look communicated the same to my father. When she looked at him in a certain way, he knew that he had better straighten up.

What education my parents had received was from a predominantly white high school in Wichita. My mother was young when I was born, and she wanted to devote herself to me instead of continuing school. So, she stayed at home and nurtured me. On the other hand, in addition to working at Boeing, my father wanted to continue with his music. He experienced lots of tension between his love of music, working at Boeing and making a living for a wife and an infant son. I was only a year old when my brother, Leander, was born. A couple of years later my mother had a third child, a daughter named Myrna. Leander and Myrna spent most of their time with our mother and father, but I spent a considerable amount of my time with my grandmother.

The three of us children were just a few years old when my father met a group of strong Christian people who had a considerable influence on his life. He went through a Christian conversion, and in many ways his life was remarkably transformed. This conversion took place in the Church of Christ, which was very conservative; some might say, even fundamentalist. They believed all the essentials of the gospel – repentance, submerged baptism, confession, faith in Christ, living a moral life, giving your money to the church and witnessing for Christ. They also believed that it was necessary for people to belong to the Church of Christ if they were to have any hope of getting into heaven. However, they did not believe in having musical instruments in the church. After attending that church for a time, he decided to become a minister. With music pulling him one way and a calling to become a minister pulling him another, he began preaching in a very small church in Pratt, Kansas.

Pratt, Kansas

I was four years old when my father began preaching in Pratt, which was a small Midwestern town with very few Black people. The church had five or six members and very few visitors on Sunday. My father played music on week nights and preached at this little church on the weekends; he was trying to make enough money, while saving souls, for us to have food and a roof over our heads. As the family drove back and forth to Pratt on the weekends, I learned the lesson of endurance.

Soon my parents began leaving me with my maternal grand-mother – Addie Sue Masters. I was born, and briefly lived, in a house across the street from my grandmother, which made it easy to visit her. Because my parents often left me with her, I became deeply attached to my grandmother. My mother wanted to be with me, but she loved my father deeply. So, she traveled with him back and forth to Pratt and I stayed with Grandma. My grandmother had a major influence on my life in those early years.

As I recall my grandmother's house, it was a "shotgun" house – the kind that you could shoot a gun through the middle of from front to back. It was a small house and when I entered the front door, I was standing in her bedroom. Beyond her bedroom, there was a large gathering room and then a small kitchen. Actually, there were only three rooms in the whole house. At the foot of my grandmother's bed there was a slop jar (also known as a combinet and defined by Webster's Dictionary as "a handled lidded pail usually made of enameled metal combining the function of chamber pot and slop jar"). Having this convenience let her get up in the middle of the night, do her business and go back to bed without going to the outhouse. My grandmother also dipped a lot of tobacco, or "snuff," and frequently spat into the slop jar.

When I was young, one of my primary jobs was keeping that slop jar emptied and keeping a small amount of water in it. I cannot express how deeply I hated that job because it was both nasty and smelly. One night I got up and heard her say, "Jerry, clean this pot out." On that occasion, I accidentally kicked over the slop jar; you can imagine the stink it left on the bed and the floor. She got a clothes hanger and hit me pretty hard and said, "Don't you ever knock that slop jar over again." I had to light the lamp, clean up the mess and then go back to my pallet on the floor in the other room.

My accidentally kicking over the slop jar and my grandmother's correction taught me a lesson that I will never forget. I learned about anger, working through anger, frustration and blame. I also learned that my grandmother loved me in spite of the serious discipline she had meted out to me. She did not beat or injure me, but she made it very clear that this was not to happen again, and it never did. I also learned that there are limits beyond which you do not go. Limits can be chains that bind you in an unhealthy way, but they can also be the source of great freedom. How many of us need to learn this lesson?

In addition to being disciplined, we did a lot of fun things as youngsters. We loved to play outside the house. We rolled tires down the unpaved streets and we caught lightning bugs in the evening and put them in jars. I'll never forget one of the myths that all of us kids knew: the myth was, "If you catch a butterfly and bite off its head, God will give you a coat the same color as the butterfly." So we tried to catch butterflies and bite off their heads and spit them out. But when I think about it now, who would want a coat the color of a butterfly's wing? Still, even simple, innocent activities can be fun!

We learned a lot of folklore in those days. For example, my grandmother, who had a very fair complexion, always drank her Hills Brothers coffee in a saucer. She poured out a bit from her cup, blew it cool and then slurped it down. I loved the smell of that coffee; I can almost smell it today. But my grandmother would never let me drink coffee. I asked her, "Grandmother, why can't I drink coffee?"

She said, "I don't want you to drink coffee because it will make you Black!" Yet, she drank gallons over the years and was far from having dark skin. I said, "Oh no, grandmother, I won't drink it, because the worst thing in the world would be to be Black." With this fear technique, my grandmother was trying to keep caffeine out of my system. Many African-Americans around retirement age or older would tell you they don't drink coffee because they were told the same tall tale – it will turn you Black. Surely that was just the folklore of Black people.

Another way of having fun was made possible by the Kansas landscape. If you know anything about Kansas, you know that people who live in the plains states experience many flash floods. Whenever the rains came, we often sat out by that unpaved road in the mud; after the downpour the street turned into a miniature river. We didn't realize how dangerous it was to sit out in the rain with thunder and lightning rolling and flashing all around us. When the rainy weather came in, my job was to make sure that the radio was not on. At the first crack of thunder, I rushed into the house and turned off our little radio. The reason for this rash action was very simple: you cannot listen to the radio when God is doing his work. And since the electricity in the sky isn't made by man, the lightning and the thunder were God doing his work up in the sky where He lived and worked. The act of turning off the radio when nature thundered gave me one of my first concepts of God, though I didn't know at the time that I was learning theology.

All of us kids sat there and watched the rain; when it was over, we ran out to play again. As we were running to the mud-holes, my grandmother would say to all of us, "Go out there and slosh in the mud!" We would go out and slosh, slosh, slosh around until we were all covered with mud. We laughed and rejoiced in that simple fun.

Through my grandmother I met all of the other people in the neighborhood. My mother's younger sister, Myrtle, lived right across the road from my grandmother's house. Aunt Myrtle also served as a surrogate parent to me. When I was growing up in Kansas, I had lots of attention, love and care that have cushioned my life until this day.

These experiences taught me manners; they made my limits and the rules for living very clear to me. I was told succinctly what I could do and what I could not do; I was taught respect for older people, especially my grandmother. I also learned that in life there are many simple things that one can do to have fun.

Though times were hard and making a living was tough, my parents never completely gave my upbringing over to my grandmother. They always loved me, and my mother told me so, but they were so stressed that my mother needed that extra help to take care of all the children.

Move to St. Louis

When I was five years old, my father was called to a church in St. Louis, Missouri. So, I began kindergarten in St. Louis, where we lived at 2626A, Madison Street. My father's little church was located at the corner of 35th and Evans Streets. Our house was certainly not in the best section of town, and neither was our church. In the apartment on Madison Street, we lived upstairs, over our neighbors, the Doakes family. Most of the Black people lived in this section of town. Though our apartment was in downtown St. Louis, the toilet was behind the apartment building, meaning that we had to go outside to go to the toilet. In those days, toilet paper was expensive to us. Instead, my mother taught me to take a page from the J. C. Penney or Sears and Roebuck catalog and rub it in my hands until it became soft. Though it didn't feel like store-bought toilet paper, rubbing it together did make it softer and more comfortable to us, especially in cold weather. I remember when I was quite young, my mother rubbed a sheet of the catalog for me, put it in my hand, and stood at the top of the steps holding the flashlight so that I could see how to get down the steps, do my business and come up again. I learned a lesson from my toilet paper experience – you can make do with whatever you have. So, stop complaining about what you don't have and use what's in your hand. I recall God telling Moses that at the Red Sea.

As children, we took a bath once a week, whether we needed it or not; and we generally took our baths in the kitchen. Back then, on the floor of the kitchen, we had an Armstrong Linoleum floor. On Saturday night, my mother took a number #10 wash tub, like we used to wash clothes in, and filled it with warm water heated on the stove. She bathed my sister, Myrna, first and that left a little dull, gray ring around the top of the tub. She then bathed Leander, my brother, and after his bath there was a second ring, just below Myrna's. Finally, by the time it became my turn to get in the tub, the water was cool and sometimes cold. My mother then added a little hot water from the teakettle to heat up my bath water. By then, the water in the tub had been used twice before it became my turn to bathe. I was the last to get a bath because I was the oldest. Cool water and a dirty ring around the tub sums up my weekly bathing experience. I learned to suck up, shut up and endure.

When I got in the tub my mother knew how I felt, but she kept saying to me, "Stop being so nice-nasty." When she finished bathing me, she would find some Murray's hair pomade and slap it on my head, then pull a stocking cap down tight, so my hair would have nice waves and would slick down. Today, not only do I avoid a bathtub, I don't wear anything on my head when I go to sleep at night. I guess I learned these preferences living at 2626A Madison Street. To be clean and look presentable doesn't require a tin tub and a stocking cap with Murray's pomade.

Taking a bath in the kitchen continues to have a negative effect on me. To this day I do not have a bathtub in my master bedroom. I can sit in a hot tub at the YMCA or take a shower in the bathroom, but I refuse to have a bathtub in my bedroom. There may be bathtubs in the house, but not in my bedroom. This is an example of how our bad memories affect our lives.

When we were younger, all of us African-American children wanted to have hair like the Caucasian people that we associated with. There were two ways that we could do it: first, we could have a conk style in which your hair was straightened, no kinks, and combed back. Nat King Cole and Sammy Davis had the conk hairstyle. The way that we achieved this straight hair was to get in the bathtub, put grease on our ears to keep them from blistering and soak our hair in lye, the kind that our mothers used to make soap. With this treatment we could have hair like the majority of the population; straight, Black and pretty like the people in the motion pictures

Not all African-American young people used lye to straighten their hair; some used Nu-Nile on their hair to get it straight and then slicked it back. We used Murray's pomade to accomplish "the look." We loaded our hair down with Murray's pomade and then put on a stocking cap. Our mothers then tied a knot in the stocking and twisted it down tight on our heads. We were very careful of how we lay on our pillows on Saturday night because we had to have our hair looking good on Sunday morning. During the week, fixing our hair didn't matter so much, but on Saturday night it was necessary because we had to be ready for church on Sunday. The next day, people at the church would look at us and say, "He's got good hair."

At our house on Saturday night, when we finished bathing, Leander and I had to grab the handles on that #10 washtub, carry it to the edge of the porch and pour the water out on the ground. And, it was made clear to us that we had better not spill one drop of bath water on that linoleum. When we finished pouring out the water, the three of us children came back into the house and climbed into a roll-away bed. When we were younger, Leander and I slept on one end and Myrna slept on the other end. As we grew up, that bed got crowded and Myrna eventually graduated to sleeping on the couch.

The little church at the corner of 35th Street and Evans had a stove in the middle of the room. On cold mornings in the winter, we put wood, and sometimes a chunk of coal, into the stove to warm the church building. I recall sitting in that little building with eight or ten older people and listening to the Jesus stories and looking at the little Sunday school cards. I suppose that all these experiences made an impression on me about religion that affected me later on.

In our family we all had tasks assigned to us. Poor folks, like us, received food from the government to supplement our food supply. I recall that we got lots of USDA peanut butter. When the box was opened, there was always a puddle of oil on the top of the peanut butter. My job was to stir it up until all the oil was absorbed throughout the peanut butter. As a consequence of stirring up that peanut butter a hundred times or more, I don't eat peanut butter today. Having to deal with all that oil and thickened peanut butter was too much for me! Once again, always know that seemingly small, insignificant things can impact who you become and what you do.

Today, I have the same feelings about oatmeal that I had about peanut butter. The government provided this cereal too. I know that oatmeal is healthy, but I still don't want any even now. The government provided us whole grain oatmeal that you had to boil fifteen or twenty minutes, not the microwave oatmeal like we have today. I suppose having something in my stomach was better than going hungry, but it made me hate oatmeal, nevertheless. My father, to make ends meet, began selling Nutrilite, a vitamin supplement. He also sold insurance to people who had very little money. Weekly he went around from house to house collecting premiums of two or three dollars – in those days it was called a debit account. My father was industrious; he preached, sold a food supplement and affordable insurance and he still had difficulty supporting his wife and three children. However, his persistence taught me endurance.

There are some things that happen to you when you are young that stay with you for your whole life. One of those experiences that stands out in my mind happened to me when we lived in St. Louis. When we arrived in St. Louis, my parents enrolled me in kindergarten at Curtis Elementary School; I did not do very well. First, I suffered from what some call being "mannish," meaning that I was always busy; I was up walking, turning, twisting, fumbling for something on my desk or another's; I was busy. Second, I stuttered. I had a very difficult time speaking to anyone, especially in the presence of a group. The teachers told my mother, who was twenty-one, that I was not doing well in the classroom. They explained to her that I stuttered, that I was always on the move, and always busy. They told my mother that they thought I was a slow learner. So they kept me back in kindergarten (I failed kindergarten, a feat not many can lay claim to). When they didn't promote me, they put me in EMR (Educationally Mentally Retarded) classes. They explained to my mother that placing me in EMR would be best for me because it would help me get over my stuttering. So I was placed in a class with those who had learning disabilities. Being labeled at an early age can be a blessing or a curse. It all depends on how you look at it.

What bothered me even more than being held back was that the next year my brother, Leander, entered kindergarten at the same school and we were in the same room. The teachers referred to me as Mrs. Durley's slow learner. I was the slow learner, Leander was the smart one. If I did anything wrong in class, the teacher pinned a take-home slip on my shirt. When I got home, my mother always asked me what I had done. Even if I wanted to avoid telling her, Leander was there to give her a full report. So when she learned how I had acted up in class, she took the ironing cord, detached it from the iron, and used it on my behind. The punishment hurt my self-esteem more than it hurt my body. She admonished me not to distract the other children, not to act out, not to talk too much and always to do whatever the teacher asked of me.

When I was in the fourth grade at Curtis Elementary School, something close to a miracle happened. We got a new teacher. One day she came up to me and said, "Gerald, da-da-da-yo-yo-you want to stop stut-stuttering? Ya-ya-ca-ca-can stop stuttering, if you just work at it." As she was saying this, I wondered to myself, "How can you stop me from stuttering, if you can't stop yourself?" I didn't say what I was thinking; I listened to what she had to say.

She then said, "I want you to come to my class and speak to my students." I went into her room and before I could open my mouth, all the children started laughing at me. Without thinking, I screamed, "I want all of you to just kiss my butt and leave me alone." My outburst came out of hurt, pain, anger, rejection, and embarrassment. Sometimes those emotions can propel you into greatness.

The teacher came over to me and said, "Did you hear yourself? You didn't stutter at all!" Although she was not always able to control her own stuttering, she taught me that people stutter because they don't know how to breathe. If you don't have the air coming at the right time, you grasp for words and wind up stuttering. By working with her and others, I learned how to relax, breathe, and control my stuttering. Listening to people who care about YOU, not your faults or weaknesses, will help you through your darkest days.

All of us have been pushed up against the wall, finding ourselves in uncomfortable spots. In life we have to find a way to respond. What happened in that class was one of the most challenging moments in my early life. I learned that you cannot run away from challenges; you must confront the situation and learn how to respond to it. After that moment in the classroom, the teachers began to look at me in a different way. My teachers asked my mother if it would be all right for them to test me to see if their original opinion held up. Of course she was willing.

After they finished with the tests, they advanced me from the fourth to the sixth grade. Quite a promotion! I was glad to be out of the same grade with my brother. This changed me, but it did not completely correct my speaking challenge. Still, when a question was asked in class, I knew the answer immediately, but I wouldn't raise my hand for fear that I would stutter when I tried to answer. I was somewhat like a person who has had a foot amputated; he or she feels that the foot is still there. That feeling matched me exactly; I felt that the stuttering was still there. But my feelings about myself were different; I now had hope. At that moment, I still retained the fear generated by the times when I tried to speak and stuttered without any control. I hoped one day to be free of stuttering. As a result, I began to withdraw and sought to avoid situations where I had to talk.

Sometimes, to take care of myself, I went out and shot basketball. This took my mind away from my struggles with speech and let me focus on something that I enjoyed. When I was playing basketball, I really didn't have to speak to anyone. I was competitive. I could take out my frustrations by being better at playing ball. There were times when I was shooting the basketball that I would say to myself, "I'm not leaving until I make three consecutive free throws." I was aware that if I could learn to shoot that ball, I could accomplish something good for myself. I continue to set short-term, achievable goals for my life, and I feel a sense of accomplishment when they are achieved. Setting achievable goals gives you confidence.

Move to Bakersfield, California 1955

When I was thirteen, my father assumed the pastorate of a small church in Bakersfield. It, too, was a Church of Christ. The church was located at 626 Butte Street in Bakersfield, and we lived in the small two-bedroom parsonage behind the church building. Five people, two bedrooms—real tight! Later, we moved into 1127 South Cottonwood Road, a three-bedroom house. This address sticks in my mind because this street was not considered to be a desirable place to live. If you asked my brother, Leander, or my sister, Myrna, they would confirm this judgment. We were all ashamed to tell our classmates that we lived on Cottonwood Road. All the excessive drinking, gambling and illicit sex took place on Cottonwood Road. If we had mentioned Cottonwood Road in the classroom, all the students would have laughed at us and made fun of us because it was the lowest end of the scale for housing in Bakersfield. Though we were in a poor section of town, we did have a water cooler on top of the house, because in the summer the temperature could get to 100 degrees and we had to have relief from the heat. We were glad to be in a larger house with an air conditioner, and we did not see ourselves as poor.

One day my father said to me, "Your mother is pregnant; she's going to have another baby." I personally didn't know about those things, so I just nodded and grunted.

He asked me, "What do you want, a brother or a sister?"

Leander and I both said, "We want a brother."

He then asked Myrna, who was three years younger than me, "What do you want?"

Myrna was quick to say, "I want a sister."

With a smile on his face, my father said, "You are all going to get what you want; your mother is having twins, a boy and a girl."

I don't know if the increase in the family caused it or not, but I felt the need to find a job and make some money, since I knew money was limited. In the summer I began work in the fields picking cotton. If I picked 100 pounds of cotton, I earned $3.50. I noticed that sometimes pickers urinated in the cotton sack to make it weigh a little heavier. If the boss caught you putting dirt clods in your sack to make it weigh more, the boss would fire you on the spot. I never did either of these nasty tricks because I would have been let go and I really needed the money. In those days Hispanics came across the river and worked with us.

Early in the morning, Leander and I got on a bus that took us out to the fields; we worked all day and at the close of day the bus driver brought us back to town. I picked cotton, cut grapes, packed tomatoes, picked peaches and sacked potatoes. When we were sacking potatoes, we had wooden stakes on our row that marked where to begin and where to end. I worked my row hard by picking up potatoes and putting them in the sack. Even in picking up potatoes and filling my sacks, I was competitive. I said to myself, "When that tractor comes back around, I'm going to have more sacks filled than anyone else." I could usually get five or six sacks of potatoes from each row that had been marked off for me.

We also picked tomatoes and placed them on a lug. A lug is a box with a handle on it so that we could put the tomatoes in it until we had it full. We got about 15 cents a lug for picking tomatoes. Whatever fruit or vegetable was in season during the summer, we were hired out to harvest it. Hard, honest, hot work will not kill you, but it will try you!

The old pickers had plenty of wisdom about picking peaches. When we picked peaches, we took a bucket with us up the ladder, filled it and brought it down and emptied it on a lug, similar to the way that we picked tomatoes. They told us young laborers that the only thing that stops the peach fuzz from itching was putting on talcum powder before you start picking. I thought they were kidding me because I was so young, but it really worked. After we had picked peaches for a few hours, our hands and face began to itch something crazy. If we hadn't treated it with talcum powder, we could have fallen off the ladder trying to scratch our skin while attempting to pick another peach at the same time.

After we had picked tomatoes for about forty-five minutes, we would get a thick film on our hands that got thicker and thicker as we picked. The crud from the vines covered our hands, and we found that the only way to get rid of the crud was by using the juice of another tomato. Every time we filled a lug or two, we had to stop and cleanse the crud off our hands with the juice of another tomato. We could always find bruised tomatoes because some had been dropped or crushed and others had been picked by birds; these damaged tomatoes did not meet the standards of the farmer. So, through the wisdom of the elders, we learned valuable lessons; talcum powder stopped the itch from peach fuzz and juice from another tomato got the crud off your hands. I learned to trust the wisdom of those who had experience in areas where I didn't, which is a big part of my success today.

In Bakersfield, we went out to the farms and picked tomatoes, grapes, and peaches. We also picked up potatoes and picked cotton. But, before it was time to pick cotton, we went to the fields and chopped cotton. The farmers always needed laborers to work in the fields, and that provided a way for me to earn a few dollars. When I finished working in the fields all day, I got on the bus and traveled back to Second Avenue in Bakersfield. There I got off the bus and walked about an hour to my house on Cottonwood Road. When Leander got old enough, he went to the field with me and helped with whatever we were harvesting. If we worked real hard and fast, we could make from $4.00 to $4.80 a day.

Working in the fields for such low wages taught me a great lesson about life. My grandmother had told me that there is nothing wrong with hard work. She said, "As long as it is good, clean, honest, and decent, there is nothing to be ashamed of in doing hard work. Be willing to do the work that no one else will do." She also taught me that "anything that is worth doing is worth doing well." We did not have much food while we worked in the fields, but we knew that the day would eventually end, and at sundown we had another day to feel good about what we had accomplished. Completing our job, making some money, and getting back home were our goals.

These same lessons apply to sports, church, community service and just about everything else. Do honorable things! Work hard! Pat yourself on the back for a job well done and prepare yourself for the next assignment!

One day, when we were not working, Leander and I went swimming. After swimming, we headed home and passed a doughnut shop that sold day-old doughnuts for 15 cents a dozen. Leander didn't have 15 cents, but I did, so I bought a dozen doughnuts. On the way home Leander asked me for one of my doughnuts, but I wouldn't give him any – not even one. I selfishly ate eight or nine doughnuts as we walked home. Before reaching the house, I had given myself a stomach ache that would not quit. When we got home, I threw up all over the front yard. Swimming in 100- degree weather and packing away a sack of doughnuts made me sick as a dog. I have never been so sick in my life. Leander, of course, was angry that I didn't share, but relieved that he didn't get sick. I learned the price of greed that day and never again have I eaten that many doughnuts. And through the pain I learned to do things in moderation. We can all learn from our mistakes.

Mr. Martin came into my life when I was in the 7th or 8th grade, just before we moved to Sacramento. He was an amateur sculptor, and he wanted to sculpt a bust of me with plaster of Paris – the kind we used to make casts to hold broken limbs in place. Can you imagine a Black boy with a bust made of white plaster of Paris? When he finished making the bust and gave it to me, he said, "The same way this plaster of Paris is solid, you can be solid in life." I, of course, did not have a clue as to what he meant. But, I accepted the bust.

I kept that bust all through my teen years, letting it remind me that I can be "solid in life" like that plaster forming my bust. I kept it until I went away to college, but I don't know what finally happened to it. Both my brother and sister were terribly afraid of that bust. They called it a ghost. Throughout my early years, and even now, the memory of that bust is a tangible reminder that my life can be solid. Mr. Martin had no idea that he would impact my life as he did. Like Mr. Martin, when we reach out to others with words or signs of encouragement, we never know what it will mean for them. Because of Mr. Martin, I have always tried to be a sower of good words into people's lives. They may not understand my positive intentions for their lives, but I am compelled to tell them, "Be the best that you can be. Make your life solid."

Sacramento, California

Our next move was to Sacramento, California where we lived on San Jose Way, not far from the stockyards. I actually attended two high schools in Sacramento: Sacramento High and McClatchy High. I still have a picture of myself in the ninth grade sitting with some fellows who played basketball at McClatchy High.

We Durley children always took our lunch to school. Can you believe we took sugar sandwiches in our brown bag lunch? When lunchtime rolled around, we were always ashamed to pull out our sugar sandwiches. In the Sacramento schools, there were a large number of Hispanic students who also brought their lunch. They usually brought frijole sandwiches – frijoles wrapped in a tortilla. We traded our sugar sandwiches for their frijoles tortillas. And when we ate them, we felt that we had gotten the best of the trade. Strangely, the Hispanic students felt the same way. Both of us were afraid to tell others what we had to eat. When I asked my grandmother about bad feelings like these, she told me, "You don't need to know anything about that. Just keep your head up and go on and you will be all right." I found it hard to be ashamed and keep my head up at the same time.

One time, I had a hole in the sole of my shoe and I felt embarrassed. I was afraid someone would see it and laugh at me. I often had a hole in either one or both of my shoes. In Sacramento I recall playing a game at school one day that required everyone to take his or her shoes off. One of my shoes had a hole in it and some of the kids laughed at me. While I was feeling embarrassed and exposed, something came to me that my grandmother taught me.

One day I told her, "Grandmother, I can't go out today."

She asked, "Why?"

I timidly explained, "I have a hole in my shoe, and I'm afraid that someone will see it and laugh at me."

She looked at me and gave me one of the greatest lessons of my life.

She said, "Bring me my quilting scissors and get me that newspaper." She folded the paper to make it thick; she then cut out a piece in the shape of my shoe and put it in the shoe over the hole. "Now put that shoe on your foot and walk across to the other side of the room," she said.

"But, grandmother, I still got a hole in my shoe!" I said.
She replied, "If you put a smile on your face, nobody will look at your shoe."

That day I decided two things: first, I would keep my head up and hope that no one would see the hole in my shoe; second, that one day I would wear the best shoes money can buy. I'm not extravagant, but I do try to buy decent clothes and good shoes; and I have no problem having them re-soled when a hole appears.

I learned over the years that it wasn't the holes in my shoes that I should've been most concerned about. There were holes in other parts of me – my character, my self-esteem, and my sensitivity. You don't recognize character-forming virtues; you let them deliver you from their opposites. Gaining these virtues is like going into a dark room and turning on the light; you don't see the darkness anymore, because it has been demolished! Virtues fill the holes in poor character.

After we lived in Sacramento for a few years, it was time to move again. I could never have imagined how our next move would provide me with new opportunities and lead to decisions that would drastically change the remainder of my life. Each time we prepared to move, I felt a hollow feeling in my gut. The thought of starting all over again and the challenge of making new friends frightened me. I now realize that each move provided me with the necessary skills to adjust to any circumstance or situation I may confront.

CHAPTER THREE

✪

I Am Amazed at How College Changed Me

FAMILY LIFE, SCHOOL AND CHURCH presented me with a variety of difficulties for the first fifteen years of my life. School in many ways was an escape, but being labeled a slow learner, struggling with my stuttering, wearing shabby clothes and bringing sugar sandwiches for lunch were sources of continuous embarrassment. By the time I was eighteen, I was disenchanted with church, at least, the kind of experiences that I had been exposed to. My father was a good man but did not attend seminary, and the faith he taught did not make sense to me. The faith that he talked about, the people who claimed to believe and practice that faith were something less than challenging examples for me to follow. It was believed that God was a big God, full of forgiveness, with a redemption plan for everyone.

From Sacramento we moved to Denver, Colorado, where my father assumed another church with the hope of earning a better living. In later years, I would often wonder where he found the courage to keep on trying to make a living in small, struggling churches. But in Denver my thoughts did not dwell on my father, but trying to adjust to another school and making the basketball team. I wanted to fit in and be accepted by my peers. We had moved so often, adjustment was central to my survival.

There were five major high schools in Denver: North, South, East, West and Manual Arts Training High School. Guess which one I went to! You're right if you said, "Manual Arts." North High was all white and socially upper class; South High had the moneyed people;

West High was made up primarily of Hispanics. East High was closest to our home. In those days each school competed vigorously with the other four in sports, social standing, and academic status.

When my father was called to a congregation in Denver, I was in the eleventh grade. At the time we thought that we were moving into an upscale neighborhood, but when I go back there now and look at where we lived, it was a very modest, humble, close-knit neighborhood. The Moses family, who were white, lived next door to us; down the street there was a Hispanic family, and a Japanese family lived across the street from us. This neighborhood was seventy percent minority, but there was a sprinkling of Asians and Caucasians. It was an authentic, lower middle income, diverse community.

I remember several guys who became my close friends: Ronnie Yamamoto, Floyd Ito and Harold Martinez. We thought nothing of our cultural differences when we played, attended classes, fought and enjoyed basketball. Yet when I reflect on those days, the Black children walked to school together, the Hispanic children walked together, and the Japanese children had their own group too. At the time we thought nothing of this obvious segregated grouping; we simply enjoyed being with people from our own distinct culture. Though we were not living segregated lives, as people were in the South, even in Denver there was a type of racial and cultural division. In those days, when my schoolmate Don McNeil dated Star Lucero, who was an outstanding Hispanic student in our school, we noticed them dating but thought nothing about it because we concentrated on other issues, like school, work and sports. It may also be interesting to note that all of our teachers were white with the exception of three. However, this ratio of white teachers and administrators was normal and accepted.

Quite a number of my classmates achieved high positions in cities across America. Notably, I went to high school with Norman Rice, who later became mayor of Seattle, Washington. Audrey Rice, his sister, ran for mayor of Oakland, California. Patsy Jo Hilliard became mayor of East Point, Georgia. So, not only do I now appreciate the excellent education from Manual High, but more significantly, the diversity within the student body.

When I lived in Denver, my best friends were Walter Hamlet and Robert Ennis. I was a struggling preacher's kid, usually wearing faded blue jeans. In those days it was not fashionable to wear ragged jeans. We pressed our worn, faded jeans and tried to make them look like new, high-priced garments. We wanted to look prosperous. It was during this time while I was friends with Walter and Robert that there was a club formed that brought together boys who were popular, smart, athletic, well-to-do and respected at the school. To be in this club, you had to dress well, be the darling of some of the girls and a macho man on campus. How could I make it? I was just a preacher's kid who didn't have the clothes, the high profile or the other requirements for membership. All I had going for me was that I was honest, tall, played ball, had a sense of humor, and was an overall nice guy.

During the club's recruitment period, guys were invited to go over to Johnny Caldwell's house on a Sunday afternoon to be introduced to the club members. Johnny was a tall, good-looking, light-skinned brother whose father owned a plumbing company. Walter, Robert and I gathered that day at Johnny Caldwell's house. Both Walter and Robert came from middle income families. Robert's mother worked at Manual High School, and his father worked on the railroad. Because they were from more well-to-do families, Walter had a 1947 Chevy and Robert had a 1957 Chevy. I could always get a ride with them wherever we were going. I never felt dependent on them; instead, I accepted the fact that they had more toys and money than I did. But, they never made me feel less than them.

On one Sunday afternoon in particular, the three of us went over to Johnny Caldwell's house. Walter was very popular. He was great at track, played football and was the captain of the basketball team. Robert was also a gifted basketball player, plus he was quite a dresser and had money. I was out of my league that day. I had none of these things, plus my jeans were faded.

That day, they interviewed us for membership, and when they came back they said to Walter, "We are happy to welcome you into the club." They said the same to Robert. Then they turned to me and asked, "You are that preacher's kid over on Humboldt Street, aren't you?" I said, "Yes, I am." They said, "It is the disposition of this body not to take you in this year, maybe next year." They obviously lacked the courage to be honest with me and tell me that they didn't believe I was socially in their class. Before this, I didn't know what it was like to be blackballed by my own people. It was all about social status, money and who you knew. That afternoon placed a sustaining brick in my foundation for life.

When they emerged from that meeting and spoke to the three of us welcoming Walter and Robert into the club, Walter stood up and said, "If Jerry cannot be part of this club, I don't want to belong to it." Robert immediately followed suit and said, "Count me out as well." I was a little dazed and confused when they stood up and said to me, "Durley, come on, let's get out of here." When I got home, I thought to myself, I don't ever want to experience that again in life. Whatever I have to do, I don't intend to be rejected like that again. I want to acquire the best and become the best at who I am and what I do. I don't ever want this feeling of rejection again. Later, when I became one of the best players on the basketball team, this group of "gatekeepers" came back to me and wanted to reconsider their vote and invite me to be a member of their club. I said, "I don't want to be a member of your club because clubs and memberships do not define who I am." I realized then that people, money and things cannot make you. Hard work, honesty and being blessed will always be triumphant.

When it came to making the decision to attend the senior prom, I still longed to be accepted. So I decided to attend. My goal was to outdress every guy at the prom, so I went downtown to buy myself a suit. I had sixty-nine dollars in my pocket and I went shopping for the best suit my money could buy. I ended up buying a hopsack suit that was an ugly pea green color. Somebody even said to me, "That's a good-looking suit." I also bought a black shirt to go with my green suit, a white tie and brown shoes. I purchased a pair of red socks, and I was ready for the prom! I couldn't wait for the night to come. I knew I was looking good when I got there. Heading over to the gym, I imagined my friends saying, "Double D, you are looking good." When I got there, I went up to a friend and waited for her to say the same, but instead she said, "You look like a Christmas tree." Initially, I thought that was a compliment. I felt Christmas trees were adorned beautifully. I went over to Walter and said to him, "This girl said I looked like a Christmas tree." He said, "You clown, she was making fun of you." With that response, my face fell and I dropped into a dark, black hole. From that experience, I learned that I should never try to impress and please everybody else. It is not what's on the outside that makes a person, but what's on the inside. Clothes will not make you—you make the clothes.

In my senior year, Manual Arts High played East High for the city basketball championship. That was the year of the 1960 Olympics. Harold Hunter was the coach at Tennessee State University, and he was a friend of Johnny McLendon. Trials for the Olympic team were being held in Denver in March and April of 1960. We won the city championship and were competing for the high school state championship. John B. McLendon, an African-American coach who would one day be inducted into the Basketball Hall of Fame, was in Denver overseeing the Olympic trials. He saw me play in the state high school basketball tournament and afterward introduced himself. I already had scholarship offers from numerous colleges across the country. Coach McLendon asked me if I had ever considered Tennessee State University. I told him that I had never heard of Tennessee State University, an all-Negro college in Nashville, Tennessee. So, I initially declined his offer because I had never been south and I was unfamiliar with the racial situation and the level of basketball talent.

Johnny McLendon asked me to consider going to Tennessee State and to play basketball under Coach Harold Hunter. Hunter was one of the coaches who had played and trained under Coach McLendon. He told Coach Hunter about me and told me that in the past year Coach Hunter had won 25 games and had an 85percent winning average during his years as a coach. To encourage me to consider attending Tennessee State, he also told me that they had a "star-studded" track team headed by Ralph Boston, a member of the Olympic team, who had broken Jesse Owens' record, a record that had stood for twenty-five years. In the 1960's Boston was best known for his broad jumping. This Black man from Laurel, Mississippi was destined to win the

Gold Medal in the 1960 Olympics and to bring credit to his school. He also told me about the TSU Tiger Belles women's track team. I was impressed. Wilma Rudolph was the star of that team.

After hearing Johnny McLendon's description of Tennessee State, its coaches and its great athletes, I made the decision to attend TSU to play basketball and to earn my degree. My parents did not fully comprehend my drive to go to college, much less a college in Nashville, Tennessee, in the heart of segregated America. Louder than the noise of their questions and fears, I felt strongly drawn to play basketball under Coach Hunter, who had been so highly recommended and to spend time in a school that had other Black people like me. It was an entirely new and different world for me, and I can honestly admit that it changed my life forever.

Freshman Year at Tennessee State University

Believe me when I say, "It is a long way from Denver to Nashville." In August of 1960 I got on a bus to ride all the way to Tennessee. I was lonely, skeptical, and afraid; not about the racial climate, but about leaving home. Then, at the Tennessee line, the driver stopped the bus. Here I was, the "Double D" (double defensive, delectable, darling, dynamic, dangerous, devastating D from Denver) being asked to go to the rear of the bus. I later learned that because of my color, I could not sit in the front of the bus. That little exercise of getting up from the front of the bus and walking to the back made absolutely no sense to me; nevertheless, I got up and made my way to the back of the bus. Little did I know, crossing that state line, I would foreshadow my destiny to spend the rest of my life fighting the injustice I had just experienced in the back of a Greyhound bus. All experiences are lessons that breed growth and development.

Rather than fume in resentment, in that moment I thought to myself, "I'm glad to have any seat on this bus because I'm going to college." I could hardly believe my thoughts, so I said it out loud, "I am going to college!" That bus ride was a defining moment in my life. I am amazed at how naïve and ignorant I was to the obvious racial discrimination I faced.

Before school got into full swing, I sat with fellow students in the student union building on a daily basis, making acquaintances and orienting myself to my new surroundings.

A group of us new students were sitting in the student union talking when the 1960 Track and Field Olympic Team came in. Among the Olympic athletes who got off the bus that day were Wilma Rudolph, Ralph Boston and the 1960 Olympic Boxing Champion, Muhammad Ali. Ali, a.k.a. Cassius Clay, had come to TSU from Louisville, Kentucky. When I thought about that moment I realized that here I was, a kid from Denver, Colorado, sitting with the champions of the 1960 Olympics. Their achievements inspired me to be my best, and one day I too would be recognized and accepted around the world.

I thanked God for Coach McLendon. He sent me to TSU. This man, who initially went to Cleveland State University as one of the first Black coaches at an all-white university, was the imaginative creator of the "fast break" in basketball. To play on his team, an athlete had to run from one end of the court to the other in four seconds. Those who did not achieve this goal had to come back and start over again and again until they did reach the four-second goal. One of Coach McLendon's rigorous requirements was that his players did not touch the basketball until they had completed three weeks of conditioning. In addition to speed, every player had to learn the basketball weave, a way of keeping the ball moving. Another exercise required each player to run to the basket, jump and touch the board, a practice that greatly enhanced rebounding. These exercises instilled in the minds of the team that basketball was a game of speed, jumping and finesse.

Chuck Taylor, a friend of Coach McLendon's, was beginning the Converse tennis shoe manufacturing company. Both to grow his company and to help his friend, Chuck Taylor came down to Tennessee State and brought tennis shoes to his friend Harold Hunter. Our team was winning titles and receiving most of the awards in our division. I loved being at TSU, playing basketball and attending classes. In all my life I had never been in a Black environment where students, professors and fellow athletes were all Black. I had never spent any amount of time with Black people who had gone to college, who had nice houses in cities like Memphis, Chicago, Atlanta and Detroit. Here, I studied with young people my same age whose parents were doctors, lawyers, ministers, teachers and business men and women. I had so much anxiety, which stemmed from my modest upbringing, that I felt like I might begin stuttering again. I told my classmates that my father was the biggest preacher in Denver, Colorado. He was far from being the biggest preacher in Denver, but could I let them be bigger and more important than I was? Could I allow myself to tell them that my daddy only had 50 to 100 members in his congregation? No! I couldn't face my lack of money, educational status, and social standing during those early years of my educational life. That would have made me appear less than. This fear, deception and fight for my ego, exposed a demon that later would have to be exorcised if I were to become who God wanted me to be.

One day our basketball team boarded a plane for New York, and I heard a directive that I had never heard before. The flight attendant's voice came across the intercom and said, "Fasten your seat belt." Like some of the fellows sitting around me, I had never been on an airplane before and I had no idea why I needed a seat belt. Honestly, none of us knew what a seat belt was. And though none of us had ever been on a plane, we acted smug and suave to fool the others as if the adventure was normal, when most us of came from meager backgrounds. I was amazed by my new environment and forgot the lessons my grandmother taught me about the hole in my shoes and putting a smile on my face. There we were, on an airplane flying to New York to play St. Bonaventure, and we were all scared to death. We had not yet learned to adapt to this strange new world of air travel.

Later, we played St. Francis College in Pennsylvania. There the local people introduced us to something new called "pizza pie." They brought us our pizza pie and when we looked at it, we didn't see a pie; we only saw cheese and dough. Where was the pie? We didn't want that cheese stuff; we wanted a piece of apple, lemon meringue or sweet potato pie. We had so much to learn. These experiences and others like them have taught me to understand how a person adjusts to new situations and accepts new experiences. I realize that the lack of ability to adjust has a lot to do with ignorance and fear. I believe that fear is based on ignorance, not stupidity, but ignorance! We fear what we do not know. I found myself sitting there in the midst of a new culture that I did not know, in a city that I did not understand and with people with whom I was barely acquainted. I can fully appreciate the phrase, "Fake it until you make it." It is critical to be open-minded when confronted with difference.

Because I did not know the background of many of my classmates, I felt ill at ease; they could have been children of a sharecropper or perhaps their father was president of a bank. After a few weeks it became clear to me that my classmates had attended predominantly Black high schools. Even though the students had attended all Black schools, they were taught by teachers who had received their degrees from prestigious white schools in the North. I had been taught by predominantly white teachers who did not have experience with the Black community. Though my high school classmates were all colors, the teachers came from a predominately white culture and background.

At TSU, the students were bi-cultural because of what their high schools taught them. Several guys on campus shocked me with a word that I had never heard. They asked me to join a "fraternity". Not knowing what a fraternity was, I immediately told them that when I fooled around with "fraternity" I usually got in trouble. I really didn't know what I was talking about. Secretly, I decided that I'd better learn what a "fraternity" was before I rejected it. I discovered that it was a brotherhood in which fellows take care of each other, support each other and provide real companionship as they faced new situations in life. I knew that I could use that kind of nurturing and support. So, I joined Kappa Alpha Psi and am a life member.

During my fourth year in college, I met a man named Dr. Samuel Dewitt Proctor. Dr. Samuel Dewitt Proctor was from Norfolk, Virginia where he was raised in a Baptist home. He was an articulate, gifted preacher and a masterful theologian in the Christian faith. He was an extremely knowledgeable man; he had a way of speaking that made his listeners remember his message. After attending Virginia State College and Crozer Theological Seminary, he became president of North Carolina A & T. While he was president of A &T, he met a young man, Jesse

Jackson, whom he took under his wing. Dr. Proctor rose quickly to being President of his Alma Mater, Virginia Union University in Richmond, Virginia. Later he received a Ph. D. from Boston University. He was so respected among young people that he was recruited to become provost at the University of Wisconsin. While he was in Wisconsin, a man named Sargent Shriver came to him and said, "My brother-in-law has started a program, and I want you to join me and become my deputy." He told Dr. Proctor that he and his brother-in-law wanted to recruit more African-American students to serve overseas. The idea for more African-American college students to serve their country abroad was something that they believed Dr. Proctor could help them achieve. It was then that Dr. Proctor became Sargent Shriver's right-hand man. He assisted in developing the Peace Corps program and after helping with the Peace Corps, he was called to serve as pastor of the Abyssinian Baptist Church, one of the most prestigious Baptist churches in America. He was called to serve the congregation of the Rev. Adam Clayton Powell, who was its former pastor. Dr. Proctor, a mentor of mine, was also a world renowned speaker, holding conferences for scores of people, many of whom he had mentored across America at every level of society.

As I became more sensitive, I began to regard my teachers and fellow students as the persons they truly were; each contributed to me, and each had a different role in shaping my identity. With a clearer perspective of myself, I began to see that people were not right or wrong, or good or bad, they were just different. We all had different parents; we were raised in different circumstances, we had different needs – we were different, and accepting diversity adds depth and interest to life. Slowly, I was beginning to make this great discovery that everyone has something to offer whether I understand it or not. My view of my peers became focused when some of them invited me to their homes during the Christmas break. I was a long way from home and I didn't have the money to buy a bus ticket to Denver. My true sense of being poor was so prevalent that I was ashamed to tell people that I did not have bus fare to go home. Going to my classmates' homes was a huge part of my permanent social education; it let me see how my peers were raised and how their parents lived. They were not poor southern Black families. They had a proud heritage. At Christmas and Thanksgiving, to cover my embarrassment, I told them I couldn't go home because the snow would be too deep and I might not be able to return to school on time. What a sad, bold-faced lie! They had never been to Denver though, so they didn't know when or how much snow we had each year. Unchecked pride can destroy the possibility of being who God wants you to be. I've learned to be honest about who I am and what I do have.

I not only experienced a rich diversity on the campus among my classmates and professors, but in Nashville I experienced a very different culture from that of Denver or Sacramento. Never before had I lived in a segregated culture. Though I had never felt the direct hostility of the racist culture firsthand, my grandmother had taught me to never allow anyone to put me in a box or label me as less than anyone else. My well-meaning teachers in St. Louis put me in a mentally retarded box; they also put me in a stutterer's box, and they put me in a box when they did not promote me. When you are born to a sixteen-year-old mother and a nineteen-year-old struggling father, people can put you in a variety of boxes, if you allow it. If you find yourself in a box, you must decide to get out of that box and create your own reality.

During my freshman year at TSU, one day in September when these new experiences were blowing my mind, I came out of the cafeteria and bumped into a group of students. Students can sometimes be very cruel to students from other parts of the country. I remember I was wearing that hop sack suit I bought for the prom in high school. It was fine for the weather in Denver in December, but not for Nashville in September. These guys stopped me and said, "Give us a light, give us a light."

I said, "I don't have any matches. I can't give you a light." They began to laugh.

While they were laughing at me a girl said to me, "They are putting you on." Then they put their cigarettes on my suit pretending to get a light, because I was wearing a winter suit in hot weather and I didn't have any summer clothes. This young woman standing off to the side told me that they were trying to make fun of me. "You need to get some lighter weight clothes," she advised.

I turned it over in my mind and decided to go to downtown Nashville and buy some summer clothes. Before leaving, I ignored what Coach Hunter had told us. He said, "Don't go downtown without someone from the campus going with you. You do not know the attitudes of white people in Nashville. " I ignored his advice because I wanted summer clothes. Shame and embarrassment forced me to go downtown alone.

I had about thirty dollars in my pocket as I headed out planning to get a seersucker coat. I went into a department store to see what I could find. As I was walking around looking for a coat, I began picking up and trying on this and that. I found a hat and put it on my head as I kept looking around the store. Then I pulled the hat off of my head and was about to lay it down when a sales lady said, "What are you doing?"

I asked her, "What do you mean? I tried this hat on and it is too small. I need a larger one." She handed the too small hat to me and demanded that I pay for it. She said, "That hat is six dollars."

I responded, "The hat's too small. I'll pay for one that is my size." I was resolute in my stance and statement.

"I'll take your money and ring it up," she said.
I thought she couldn't hear, so I bent down and spoke louder, "The hat is too small for me."

About that time, a man came up and asked, What's the problem?" I told him that she had demanded that I pay for a hat that doesn't fit me. She immediately interjected, rather loudly, "He won't buy this hat." Once again, I stated firmly, "Ma'am, the hat's too small." Then I asked, "Who is in charge?"

"Get the manager," the woman shrieked. A crowd swelled around us. I hadn't seen all of the people, because I was so angry.

The manager appeared and said, "You can't ask this boy to pay for something he doesn't want. That's not the policy of this store." I felt relieved and vindicated.

Then he asked the sales clerk, "What's the problem?"

She explained, "He tried this hat on and then sought to replace it on the shelf."

The manager asked, "Why did you want to put it back on the shelf?"

I said, "I tried it on my head and it was too small."

He snatched the hat out of my hand, slapped me across the face with it and said, "Nigger, who is going to buy that hat after it has been on your wooly head?"

Then and there, I was baptized into blatant racism at its highest degree. They took the money out of my pocket and literally threw me and the hat out on the sidewalk. The other customers showed their mass approval with thunderous applause and laughter. My life was changed forever.

I wandered back to the campus with a bruised ego, walked up to the coach's house and said, "Coach, I'm leaving. I've got to get away from these mean, nasty people." Then I told him the story.

He said, "I told you not to go downtown by yourself."

I said, "I'm leaving and I'm not going to discuss it anymore."

In a disgusted tone he said, "Go on home, just go on home. Give up on your future." I told him again what had happened to me at the department store. I kept saying to myself, "I've got to leave; I will get killed here." When pain confronts you, ask yourself, is the pain going to prevent me from achieving my goals? The answer is NO!

I walked out of the coach's house and it dawned upon me that I couldn't go home. I didn't have enough money to buy a ticket to Chattanooga, much less to Denver. Suddenly it occurred to me that it was time for basketball practice and I had to rush to the gym. Even though I told Coach Hunter I was leaving, I knew that if I was late, I could not practice and the coach would throw me off the team. I had never been cut from or dismissed from a team in my life. So I rushed over to the gym, put on my athletic clothes and gave practice my best. That's just who I am. I didn't intend to get cut from the team, lose my chance for an education at another college, then have to hitchhike to Denver. Being broke, I didn't have any other way of getting home, so I went to practice as usual. It was a painful day.

Introduction to the Civil Rights Movement

After practice, when I got back to my dorm room, there was a note on my door saying "Join us at Fisk University." The note promised there would be some men at Fisk who had come to Nashville to inform the Black students at Fisk and Tennessee State regarding life issues that negatively impacted Black students. So I went to Fisk and met four guys who were talking about fighting against segregation and learning more about social justice issues. Two of them were about my same age. I was impressed! Before that evening, I had never heard of any of those men and knew less about segregation and social injustice against Black folks. They wanted to organize, in Nashville, a movement of Black students who would take part in challenging the injustices that we were facing. After my hat experience in the department store, I was a prime prospect for the Civil Rights Movement. But, I felt that I could not join the movement because I was a basketball player and we had been instructed not to get involved in any controversial organizations. The college recruited us to play basketball, not protest.

A few days after I had been thrown out of the department store, I was ready to hear about any and all efforts to prevent anyone from going through what I had endured. I craved knowing how change could come about. I didn't understand what occurred in the department store; I didn't know what I had done wrong. Confusion reigned in my mind! The men I met at Fisk emphasized that the movement would not tolerate fighting, cursing or violence. It was going to be a non-violent movement. They were advocating a firm but peaceful movement. What a challenging, earthshaking year my first year in college had been!

One night a group of us students were organized to go to a movie theater. As we were standing in line, I witnessed, first-hand, the spitting and hitting from whites that we had been warned against. Our organizers forbade any kind of reactive behavior; our parents had strongly discouraged our getting involved with any violent protest. Week by week, I was becoming more exposed to different ways of responding to the hate of racism. While my interest in these forms of protest grew day by day, I was also trying to find a way that I could personally survive in college without money. I had to preserve my scholarship. I couldn't lose my room, board, tuition and opportunity to play professional basketball. I was compelled to stay the course, and get involved.

After the summer ended, I came back to Nashville for my second year of college. That year I became one of the student leaders on the campus. I brought variety in my approach to leadership on the campus. My style had been shaped by my life experiences: I had risen from poverty, I had defeated loneliness and I began to make fast friends with other students. After my first year on campus I also received recognition for my varsity basketball experience, my service to others, my grades and my personal friendships. My leadership continued through the first three years at TSU, and at the end of my junior year my classmates elected me president of the student body.

After three years in school, I became much more involved in the Civil Rights Movement. In 1961, the bus carrying the Freedom Riders departed Nashville. I wanted to go with the Freedom Riders. That afternoon, I went to basketball practice in the afternoon and as soon as practice finished, I ran to the dormitory where the bus was departing from. Unfortunately, or maybe fortunately, I missed the bus. The Freedom Riders' bus was met at the state line; students were pulled off the bus, harassed and arrested. Then the segregationists burned the bus. After that catastrophe, I vowed that whatever profession I wound up in, I would be working to create a healthy environment whereby people could develop into their best without discrimination and hatred blocking their way.

I tried to understand why certain white folk were so mean and cantankerous. In those days, even the good white people were invisible to us. Though they were so close, we could not see them. If white people had really looked at Black people, they would have realized that we were the most conservative group in America. We were taught to work hard, keep our noses clean, get a good education, be on our best behavior. Our leaders emphasized to us that we were to stay out of trouble and to respect our elders. But the white community flipped the switch on us when it came to integration. Suddenly, hard working, respectful Blacks were demanding and pursuing social, educational and legislative changes that challenged well-established customs; they were insisting on justice in the public arena, and white people found it difficult to honor our demand for freedom and justice.

In the summer of 1963, I again went to Camden, New Jersey

where, for several summers, I had worked and played basketball. In August of that year I learned that there would be a national March on Washington, D.C. The March on Washington represented a coalition of several civil rights organizations, all of which had different approaches and different agendas. The coalition included the Congress of Racial Equality (CORE), the Southern Christian Leadership Conference (SCLC), the Student Non-violent Coordinating Committee (SNCC), the Brotherhood of Sleeping Car Porters, the National Association for the Advancement of Colored People (NAACP), the National Urban League and numerous other labor and youth groups.

I planned to attend with several of my friends and to participate in the protest. We got to Washington about 9:00 a.m. the day of the march. When we arrived, there may have been only 25,000 people assembled at the Lincoln Memorial. The march was organized to get the attention of the nation around voting and civil rights. As we wait-ed for the speakers to begin, more people came and by the time that Martin Luther King, Jr. spoke to the crowd there were 250,000 people enthralled by his words. Martin's speech that day changed my life and the attitudes of many others across America. What I saw, felt and heard that day marked me forever and has become the foundation for most of my life decisions.

Jumping ahead a couple of decades, I had an experience apropos of this day. A few years ago Mrs. Coretta Scott King and a group of us were laying a wreath on Dr. King's tomb when she told us what had occurred the night before that famous speech. She described how on the night of August 27, 1963 at about 10:00 p.m. Martin found out that because there were a number of groups sponsoring the march, he would have only twelve minutes to speak to the crowd. She relayed to us that Dr. King always wrote out what he would speak. He spent all night writing and rewriting his speech, trying to get it just right. He wanted it to be precise and clear. He finished his revisions about 5:00 a.m. on the day of the march. The crowd swelled with people com-ing from all over the nation. When it came time for him to speak, the facilitator said, "Dr. King, this is the crowd which we had anticipated; speak as long as God leads you." Dr. King gave more than the speech he had worked on all night. Few people even recall very much of what he said the first eight minutes, but we all remember the conclusion of the speech. Dr. King spoke with an anointed, prophetic voice, insightful wisdom, power, passion, purpose and love.

The ending is what people recall from the "I have a dream" speech. There are *chronos* moments and there are *kairos* moments, and this was a *kairos* moment – when things came together that were not planned. It is a *kairos* moment when God speaks. At times when all the things around us cave in on us, there will come a *kairos* moment in our life that will deliver us from all fear and doubt. *Kairos* does not depend on minutes and hours, but comes unexpectedly when the Spirit breaks through on us. When *chronos* time overpowers our actions, *kairos* negates the pressures of the moment.

After the speech was finished, my friends and I got in the car and went back to the campus to become more committed to voter registration. The other fellows were registering in the churches; however, during that period of my life, I was not that involved in the church. I had had church dogma up to my eyeballs and I was disenchanted with the church as I knew it.

Following the historic march and the increasing emphasis on voter education and registration, a crisis event occurred in Dallas, Texas — on November 22, 1963 John F. Kennedy was killed. As students we asked, "What does this mean? Where will the movement go now?" I was confronted with the huge task of speaking to the student body at Tennessee State about the impact of President Kennedy's assassination. What was I to say? I asked my peers, as well as myself, "How do we move ahead with the vision?" The loss of John F. Kennedy created a leadership vacuum in our minds and a great deal of confusion as to what would happen to the Civil and Voting Rights Movements. We felt that we needed a renewed source of support and guidance in planning our next steps. His death was also a major event that made us more determined to make Dr. King's prophecy a reality. Dr. King was a leader and a source of strength, but President Kennedy, we felt, gave us political courage.

The Peace Corps

With apprehension covering the movement like a ground fog, I was sitting in Clement Hall on the campus of Tennessee State when a Black man, Dr. Proctor, whom I have previously mentioned, came into my room with a white man whom I did not know. Dr. Proctor told me, "The president of the college, Dr. Walter Davis, said, 'If you want to address the student body, you have to talk with Gerald Durley, who is president of the student body.'"

So Dr. Proctor said to me, "I would like for you to meet this man; I think he can make a difference in your life." I was personally in no mood to introduce a white man to the student body. Our capacity for tolerating whites was extremely low.

I said, "No, I don't want to be bothered."

Dr. Proctor emphatically pressed on, saying, "I want you to meet this man. The president said that if you consent, you may introduce this man to the student body."

With a bit of sarcasm and disrespect, I said, "No, I have no interest in meeting or introducing him to our students." I didn't appreciate a Black man bringing this white man into my room after all we had endured from a "white-controlled" system. King's "I have a dream" speech and the assassination of President Kennedy were still fresh in my mind, and these feelings were influencing my reaction to Dr. Proctor's extremely sincere request.

Then he inquired further, "May I ask you three questions?"
In my belligerence I retorted, "You can't ask me anything. I'm not interested in any questions you may have of me."

But he persisted, saying, "There are three questions that I want you to answer. I am going to ask them to you and if you wish not to answer them, I'll leave you alone and you will not have the responsibility of introducing this man tomorrow."

He asked, "Who do you know? Who do you know that is important? Do you know the mayor of this city?" His questions made me feel like he was putting me down in front of this white man; I felt anger boiling inside me.

Then he asked, "How much money do you have? I mean real

money, in your pocket? "

I answered, "About thirty-six or thirty-seven dollars."

He proceeded, asking, "Where have you traveled outside of the USA? (At this point I was certain he was putting me down, but I was pleased to answer his third question proudly and loudly).
"I have been to Hawaii," I said.

He immediately responded, "I asked where you've traveled outside of the USA."

I became angry, embarrassed, and hurt. I felt myself going back to the feeling I had when I asked my grandmother about the hole in my shoe.

Dr. Proctor said, "I don't mean to insult you. But according to your answers, you don't know anyone important. You don't have any money, and you have never seen the world. Why don't you at least listen to this man? His late brother-in-law, President Kennedy, created a program, the Peace Corps, that you and the student body might be interested in exploring for your future."

He looked me straight in the eye and said, "Let me introduce you to Sargent Shriver. We would greatly appreciate you introducing him at tomorrow's assembly. He will briefly discuss his program."

I shook hands with Sargent Shriver, and the next day I introduced him to the student body of Tennessee State University. He spoke with such power and integrity about the Peace Corps that I promised him that upon graduation I would enroll. I graduated in June 1964 and went to Peace Corps training at Central State College in Wilberforce, Ohio from June through July. I left for Eastern Nigeria, West Africa in August to serve my country.

The Influence of TSU on My Life

A number of persons made lasting impressions on me while I was in school at Tennessee State University. Among those were Dr. Nathaniel Crippens, Mr. Murrell, my dorm manager, Coach Howdy Green, Coach Harold Hunter and Dr. Calvin Atchison. Dr. Nathaniel Crippens was the registrar at TSU. He was a top educator and one of the most brilliant people that I've ever met. Dr. Crippens was always there for me during my darkest moments. He was my primary advocate when my schoolwork was a little tardy or I missed a class or I was simply too busy playing basketball. He was always there to tutor and counsel me, when I didn't know that I even needed advice.

One outstanding memory that I have of Dr. Crippens was his response to our President's giving financial aid money back to the state. Our president, Dr. Walter S. Davis, remitted more money back to the state than Middle Tennessee State University, the University of Tennessee or East Tennessee State University. In my mind, TSU could least afford to give this money back. At that time, I was president of the student body when I saw on the front page of *The Tennessean*, the city newspaper, a picture of the governor giving our president a prize bull. Of course, people wanted to know if he was currying up to the governor by giving back the financial aid in order to get a prize bull. Some reporters from the newspaper came to me and asked me, as the president of the student body, "What do you think about your president giving money back to the state, and receiving a prize bull?" I said, "That's a lot of bull!" Dr. Crippens thought it was inappropriate for the president to return money to the state when so many of us were dependent upon it for our school expenses. Without the help of Dr. Crippens and Dr. Atchison, I could not have remained in school. The two of them got together with other faculty and contributed enough money to pay my tuition for my final year. I believe that honesty and truth will always reward those who follow their virtues.

Mr. Murrell was also a strong advocate and friend. He was the dorm manager and he often said to me, "Durley, you need to watch out because the president is not pleased with your response to the news media." When Mr. Murrell was issuing his warnings, I was organizing the dorm to buy enough Marlboro cigarettes to win a free TV for our dorm. Even in college, I was always organizing something. I sought to get everybody I knew to buy Marlboro, so we could acquire enough recognition to win the television set. I was even asking students who didn't smoke to buy packs of Marlboro so we could win. Mr. Murrell was always looking over my shoulder to keep me out of more conflicts with the administration.

And then there was my "Coach", Howard Green, who was another strong influence on me. He was from Pennsylvania and was a no nonsense coach who grew up around white people and understood their culture. He didn't want any Black people, like us, to ever be less than who we were. Howdy Green attended my wedding; he was a true and lasting friend. Several years ago, I had the opportunity/responsibility to conduct his funeral – a very sad day in my life, but those who touch and change our lives never really die; their memories live on forever.

Harold Hunter was also a mentor to me; he was the first Black man to play professional basketball. His starting salary was $4000 a year. Harold was only 5'8," but he played as tall as any six footer. He died at the age of 86. I had the honor of conducting the eulogy and learned that his wife, who was our queen, had Alzheimer's. At his funeral, I stood beside guys who played with the Harlem Globetrotters and other professional teams. By the time of Harold's death they were all up in years. But, these old pros flew in from across the country just to honor the man who had changed their lives and enabled them to make a decent living playing basketball. I was the only one among them who was a preacher. Occasions like those always seem to amaze me, and leave me to ponder why I was the chosen one.

Dr. Calvin Atchison, my advisor, also had a powerful influence on me. When I initially went to college, I thought I wanted to be a medical doctor. Dr. Atchison was a psychologist who understood my inner workings better than I did. He said, "No, Jerry, you have too many skills to go into the medical field; you would waste a number of your gifts." He acknowledged that medicine was a noble profession, but he felt that I was a people-person and that I needed to choose a vocation that kept me close to people. He, along with all the others, had a very lasting impact on all of my life. They each contributed to who I am.

While I was being molded by these strong leaders, my mother and father remained in Denver. After the first three children were born, they had three more, and taking care of these three younger children kept them occupied. My mother volunteered for the Head Start Program. Though she did not finish school, she surely knew the value of an education for Black kids. When she applied for this job, the doctors discovered that she had cancer. Without the physical examination required to work with the children in the Head Start Program, she might never have known about the cancer. As a consequence of that, I have been willing to go anywhere to speak about the Head Start Program in honor of my mother. My father continued to pastor the Church of Christ in Denver, Colorado. My younger brother, Leander, set the high jump record at the University of Colorado, but then he dropped out of school in order to pursue his love for music. While I was in college, my younger sister, Myrna, got married and began raising a family. Attending college at Tennessee State meant that I could not go home for one single summer. When I left Denver, I virtually left my family. Circumstances dictated that it was time for me to grow.

Going to college at Tennessee State University has meant everything to me. When I went to college, I was extremely naïve, transparent, open, honest and easily fooled. I was all of these things because I wanted to be liked and to fit in with the crowd. I didn't want to step on anyone's feelings and, consequently, I was seemingly always getting hurt. I had a kind of blind trust in everyone I met because I didn't know how to listen with my third ear – the ear that hears what is meant, not what is said. I was not very wise about the thoughts and behavior of girls; I played basketball and studied, but in my sophomore year, I was inducted into Kappa Alpha Psi Fraternity, Inc. Initially, I more or less drifted with the flow of college life because I had no real role models.

I realized at the end of my first school year why my coach and my advisors sought to keep me from situations like going downtown; they knew the rejection that I would face as a young Black man. I could have been locked up or lynched. I mistakenly thought they were trying to impede my progress and growth by keeping me on campus. After these learning experiences, I began to listen with that third ear—the ear that hears what is really meant. In those days, I had great difficulty with President Davis, but today I honor, respect and revere his memory in spite of the Governor's gift of a prize bull. He was able to keep a Black college solvent even during segregated times. By the end of my college years, I was beginning to develop a stronger appreciation for myself and who I had become in relation to the larger world. I left college with an excitement about the world, about life and about the possibilities that presented themselves to me. My experience at Tennessee State enlarged my vision and sharpened my faculties to enter into adult life with a richer, broader world view. I learned that everybody has an agenda; I can either endorse their agenda or reject it, but that does not mean that I reject the person. Everyone has value, and I must respect who they are even if we are vastly different.

Stumbling Through Graduation

One thing that stands out in my mind about graduating from Tennessee State University is overcoming an "F" I received my freshman year in ROTC. Near the end of my days at TSU, this incident was marked indelibly in my mind. When I enrolled at Tennessee State University, each male was required to finish three quarters of ROTC. During one of the first quarters, I was so involved with basketball that I missed a class which I never made up and thus received no credit for that quarter. When it came time to graduate, I did not have sufficient credits in ROTC to walk across the stage and receive my degree. I went to talk with Colonel Baugh, who was head of ROTC training at TSU. I was in my senior year and I had to work out a plan with Colonel Baugh to get my degree. I had a 3.8 out of a 4.0 GPA, and I had been offered fellowships by both The Woodrow Wilson and The Danforth Foundations. I was on the varsity basketball team, and I was the president of the student body and I was still being told that I could not graduate without the third quarter of ROTC. My coach, Howdy Green, and my advisor, Dr. Calvin Atchison, told me to make an appointment with Colonel Baugh. They were endeavoring to help me clear my record so that I could graduate on schedule.

I went down to Colonel Baugh's office and sought to schmooze my way through the problem. My verbal tricks did not work!

Colonel Baugh asked me, "What is it, Mr. Durley?"

"They said that I cannot complete graduation because I have an F as a grade for one quarter of my ROTC, and I really do want to graduate."

Colonel Baugh asked, "What's the problem?"

I said, "If you remember, sir, we were traveling a lot in basketball and I was busy and had to study to make my grades and I failed to come to ROTC the proper number of times."

The Colonel said, "That is not an acceptable excuse! When you signed up for this course, you knew that there was an attendance requirement." That was another great lesson of my life. When you commit to a project, complete it and do it well.

I began to make other excuses and tried to debate my way out of my mess, but the Colonel said that there was no way to erase the F from my record.

He said, "Yes, you can graduate, if you retake the course and pass."

I said, "You would keep me from graduating from college for one hour of ROTC? I'm not even going into the Air Force. I really could not care less about the Air Force."

"Then stay here for another quarter, because you will not graduate." Those were Colonel Baugh's words of encouragement.

After this conversation, the President of the University talked with Colonel Baugh. He advocated on my behalf and then told me to go back and talk to Colonel Baugh again. In retrospect, this is an example of how Dr. Davis was a great champion for student rights. At the time, I was too myopic and self-absorbed to see his strong integrity.

I went back to see Colonel Baugh a second time and he said to me, "I'll give you a chance to make up the grade." I felt great appreciation for his compromise. Colonel Baugh continued, "I want you to take an M1 rifle and walk around the quarter mile track thirty times with it on your shoulder."

I said, "Colonel Baugh, that is asking too much. It is hot in Nashville in May."

Again, he said, "Do you wish to graduate or not? Either walk around the track with the M1 rifle or your grade will remain an 'F' and you won't graduate."

I talked with Dr. Atchison, my academic advisor, and he said, "What is your goal? What are you trying to accomplish? What are you aiming for? Don't ever forget your goal. What do you lose by walking around that track thirty times?" His comments taught me to learn to compromise to achieve one's desired goals. Keep your integrity, but don't ever lose sight of your goals.

I subsequently went down to the track the next Saturday morning. Colonel Baugh gave me an M1 rifle, then sat down in the bleachers and counted my laps around the track. Halfway through, I heard him yell, Fifteen, and a little later, Eighteen. I stayed with it until I had completed thirty laps. The accomplishment of completing my goal to graduate by walking those laps taught me discipline.

When I finished walking around that track, Colonel Baugh said, "Mr. Durley, I cannot give you an A, but I will give you a C, which means you have completed the course." The goal was not a grade, but the opportunity to graduate. I define my desired outcomes clearly now and will sacrifice to accomplish them.

And still today I have a grade of C for ROTC on my TSU transcript. But, the Administration allowed me to graduate.

Never lose sight of the broader goal and only quit when victory has been won. Thank you, Colonel Baugh, Dr. Davis, and Dr. Calvin Atchison.

CHAPTER FOUR

✪

I Am Amazed at the World I Discovered

WHEN DR. SAMUEL DEWITT PROCTOR came to my dormitory room in 1964, I had no idea how that visit would change my life. That afternoon I met Sargent Shriver and agreed to introduce him to the student body the next morning. That decision was a turning point in my life. Before that afternoon, if I had been asked to join the Peace Corps and go to Nigeria for two years and work with a bunch of African farmers, I would have said, "No way! Not on your life!" But we never know when the Lord will speak and what decisions we will make when the Spirit challenges us. Dr. Proctor challenged me with those three questions and Sargent Shriver challenged me to accept a marvelous opportunity. Always open the door when positive opportunity knocks. Joining this program, entitled the United States Peace Corps, created an emotional conflict within me. At the time, Black students were in the middle of the Civil Rights struggle and we were not concerned with supporting the United States government; we had no desire to leave the country or abandon our role in the movement. I had been working hard to complete my college degree, so serving in another country with no salary made absolutely no sense at all. I did not understand the initial impact of Dr. Proctor's three questions to me. Those questions suggested to me that maybe I should at least expose myself to a broader world. The next day Sargent Shriver made his presentation about the Peace Corps to the students of Tennessee State University. It was January of 1964.

As I listened to Sargent Shriver the following day, something inside of me was altered. Though I was deeply committed to Civil Rights and equally concerned about the role of African-American students in the movement, I realized that there was a broader world beyond America that offered larger experiences and new visions. I knew that after I left college, I would encounter a much different world than I had been exposed to during my college days. After my term as student government president, I continued to be involved in the student movement, but I felt drawn to the US Peace Corps. When I graduated from college, I had already filled out the paperwork to join.

Peace Corps in Nigeria

After graduation from Tennessee State, I was sent to Central State College in Wilberforce, Ohio. At Central State I began an intensive training program. We were labeled 'Nigeria Peace Corps Group Twelve.' The International Assistance Program was designed to assist with developing youth programs and improving agricultural crops. Our team was the first group of Peace Corps volunteers to go into rural Nigeria to work with youth and farmers. My role in Nigeria was to make an effort to get protein into the diet of young people by increasing egg production. We began "Young Farmers Clubs" to create a base from which to work. These clubs offered information and support in the application of new methods of farming, poultry production and increasing egg supply.

Nigeria had gained independence from Great Britain in 1960. Four years later, we were there offering a program which was important to Nigerians because they sought improved methods to produce food, both for their own people and for exportation. One of the primary roles of the Peace Corps, when it first started, was to help countries develop and build a relationship with the US government. Our group of Peace Corps workers traveled to Lagos, a port city and the largest city in Nigeria. All the cities in Nigeria were exploding with young people coming in from rural areas, seeking jobs.

Preparation and Travel to Nigeria

When I went into Peace Corps work, I met other young people

from across the nation who were also interested in serving the needs of people. Most of these were young, white people who could have afforded to take trips to Europe or anywhere else they wanted to travel, but they had chosen to do Peace Corps work and were sent to Nigeria. I often wondered why they were willing to take on the tasks that we were being trained to perform. I also questioned myself; why was I going to Nigeria, when we had a movement underway that I desperately wanted to be part of?

One of the young men that I met in Wilberforce, Ohio was David L. Crippens, the son of one of my advisors at Tennessee State. He proved to be a good friend and through the intervening years, we have remained in touch with each other. When we got on the plane to go to Nigeria, I had a feeling of excitement and great expectations about what those two years would be like.

My first impression of Nigeria came when we boarded the airplane in Frankfurt, Germany to fly to Lagos, Nigeria on their national airline, where for the first time in my life I saw a Black pilot step out of the cockpit. Not only was there a Black pilot, but for the first time I saw Black stewardesses. I've never seen a pilot with a greater smile on his face than the man in that striking uniform. I did not know Black people flew airplanes. What an enlightening moment.

When we landed in Nigeria, I saw nothing but Black people; when I looked up at a billboard, I saw a big, Black face smiling at me and saying that we should be drinking a certain kind of drink. He had a Black baby in his arms. All the police officers and taxi cab drivers were Black. Over the course of training, I had become closely acquainted with three other Peace Corps workers: David Crippens of Antioch College, Tom Morgan of Howard University and James Bartley, who had attended Bethune-Cookman College. As we entered the hotel where the Peace Corps had reserved rooms for us, all the greeters at the door were Black. The bellman, the clerks behind the desk and the owner of the hotel were all Black. Everything and everybody was Black. I experienced culture shock as I watched them and marveled at their ability to speak two or three different languages.

The white Peace Corps workers had a similar experience. Many of them had been to London and Paris, but being in the minority was entirely new for them. They, too, had never experienced a preponderance of Black people in a Black country. I find it difficult to describe my experience. Realizing that all of the people around me were Black was a situation that I had never experienced before. Seeing all of those Black people in leading roles made me ask myself how I could leave the United States when the Civil Rights Movement was just beginning to gain momentum. From Lagos, they put me in a lorry (the British refer to a truck as a lorry) and transported me over the mountain, across a large river, and down the hill to Eastern Nigeria, my home for the next two years.

Postcard Incident

Two groups of Peace Corps workers went to Nigeria: those who were trained to work in agriculture and those who were primarily teachers. My group had an agricultural focus. Our efforts concentrated on farming, specifically, producing farm products that put more protein in the diet of the people. During our training, we had been briefed that the culture in Nigeria would be very different from the culture in the U.S., and we were taught to be accepting of those differences. We too were learning as we attempted to teach others. We understood that our primary function was to establish and nurture relationships. One of the white volunteers who was a teacher, with a focus on English as a second language, caused a significant scandal when she wrote and mailed a postcard back home describing the conditions in Nigeria. Her postcard described poor, dirty children running around naked and barefoot, with uncombed hair. She wrote it on a two-sided open postcard and sent it through the Nigerian mail. Nigerians in the post office intercepted it and vehemently complained to the State Department that if this was what the Peace Corps did, they wanted no workers in Nigeria. The incident was eventually smoothed out and we stayed, but we were again lectured by our leadership that we were not to speak disparagingly about the people we were serving.

My Nigerian friends

I made two special Nigerian friends – Titus Nwadioha and Mr.

Odu, who were helpful to me in every way. Mr. Odu was the District Manager of the Department of Nigerian Agriculture, and his job was to teach me how to plant palm oil trees. The government gave us the palm oil trees, and we were to teach the local people how to plant, care for and harvest palm oil. The government also furnished us with chickens, which we distributed in the villages to provide more protein derived from the eggs and chicken meat, which they ate. I went to the villages and talked with the people about chicken and palm oil production. The real emphasis of the Peace Corps was on creating communication between the people of the village and us Americans. This is when I began to feel compelled to form Young Farmers Clubs in my village.

The Young Farmers Club

A particular member of the Young Farmers Club was named Titus, a person I well remember. There is a funny story about this young man. He and I were paired together to do land surveying. When I was using the survey equipment, I would tell him to move to the left or to the right. He would always say, "Who me?"

I said to him, "Titus, we are the only ones here. You don't have to ask, 'who me?' When I ask you to move the chain, you just move it." He said, "Okay, okay, I got it."

Immediately, I said, "Titus, come a little closer."

Invariably, he still said, "Who me?"

When we got through working, Titus and I walked among the palm trees and drained some of the juice, put a few wood chips in it and brewed some of the finest wine you have ever tasted. Palm wine was sweet, cost very little, and was strong!

All of us Peace Corps workers had motorbikes. We often put some of the natives on the back seat and rode through the village. Riding through the village on the back of a motorcycle gave them a thrill and increased our personal bonds of friendship.

The villages also had repairmen: one man repaired clocks, another bicycles and still another motorcycles. One of these repairmen came up to me and said, "My name is Daniel." He continued, "You are the tallest man I have ever seen and I love tall people. In my village when you are tall, you are somebody." I thanked him and we drank some palm wine together. On another day he came to me and said, "Jerry, I need you to do me a big favor."

I asked, "What is it?"

He said, "Everybody in this village sees me as only a bicycle repairman, but I want to be somebody that is highly respected. The way I can do that is to have a tall, strong son, just like you."

I was following his logic at first, but then he asked, "Will you chu, chu, chu with my wife?" And I realized that he was asking me to impregnate his wife.

"What did you say?"

He replied, "I said, would you chu, chu, chu with my wife so that I could have a baby that will grow up to be big and tall like you?" He had a young wife who was attractive, but who questioned sleeping with me, even if her husband gave his permission. I never once considered his request.

Furthermore, our Peace Corps training had warned us not to have any sexual encounters because of the potential for creating a negative image of Americans. However, when I declined his offer, Daniel felt rejected by me. He told everybody in the village that I had embarrassed him and made him feel terribly bad; and he became quite angry and was vocal about what had transpired. This incident taught me how to be culturally sensitive and graciously decline a request in a different culture.

Daniel said to me, "You think you're too good for us. You're too good for our women. You will not give me a son?"

I said, "No, no, that is not true."

Finally, I was able to get the chief to bring us together to let me explain the situation. I tried to help him understand that in our culture, we did not impregnate other men's wives, and furthermore, as a Peace Corps worker, I could not respond to his request. This was my introduction to a different culture with different norms.

All Peace Corps workers had a local person to work with us. I lived in what they called a DO's (District Officer) house. This was a one-bedroom house with an outdoor toilet; every night I had to sleep under a mosquito net for protection. I cooked what I wanted to eat, and there was not very much cleaning up after having breakfast. As a U.S. government employee, I went out to villages to explain the various programs that we were offering them through the government. I explained how raising chickens and planting palm oil trees would improve their health and provide financial resources. If we could get them to plant enough trees, the government would buy the oil from them. The chickens could immediately change their lives by laying eggs that could be sold in the market place. We taught them about the nutritional value of the protein in the eggs. I also learned a lot about their food and its value.

The villagers would gather us all together in the evening to cook. Occasionally, we would roast a whole pig. I often took James Brown records with me for listening and dancing. I also formed a singing group that entertained in the villages. We sang and danced to Chubby Checker's music. James Brown was also one of our favorites. At these village parties I stood with a microphone in my hand, singing and entertaining, which kept us laughing and having great fun. When people laugh, eat, drink, dance, work, and worship together, there are very few differences among them.

I also worked with another volunteer named Bill Campbell; his expertise was engineering wells for water. He went from village to village, helping to locate, pump and purify the water. He also helped with irrigation implementation plans and other ways toproperly water crops. While I was assisting people in the village, I never forgot that my purpose was to be a positive influence as we talked about American culture and Nigerian culture. The significant impact of our being there as the Peace Corps was to establish relationships with the Nigerians and give them a positive image of America. I'll never forget, when I was ready to leave, the chief said to me, "Your departure makes me feel like a man being bitten all over by mosquitoes, and that is the pain I feel with your leaving. It hurts all over." He further explained, "When you leave, Jerry, we want you to leave for good, not for bad." I said, "Yes, I want to leave for good and not for bad, too."

I felt that the Young Farmers Club would keep many of the children who were wandering to the cities closer to home and to the land. This not only minimized the growth of the cities, it helped young people avoid many of the temptations that abounded in the cities. For two years I established Young Farmers Clubs, working under the direction of the Ministry of Agriculture in Nigeria. Along with social programs, we introduced basketball and other sports programs, exposing the young men to another exciting American sport. For me it was especially important to share with them some of the goals of the Civil Rights Movement. Many of the African young people wondered what life was like for a young African-American male fighting for the right to vote. They wondered what the challenges were in the USA around finding housing and employment. I had an opportunity to share information with numerous Nigerians, not only about agriculture, but also about the life of a Black man in America. These discussions may have been my most important contribution during my two-year stint.

I went to Nigeria in 1964 for a two-year project. The atmosphere was relatively calm when I was there, but in 1967 the southeastern provinces of Nigeria, which had economic, cultural and religious conflicts with the northern provinces, sought to secede from the union and form a separate country. The conflict lasted for about three years, and I was thankful that I left before it escalated into a civil war. After I served my two years in Nigeria, some of the members of my Peace Corps group elected to serve in other countries.

I was somewhat concerned with a personal matter during the last year of my Peace Corps term. That year I wrote to several colleges and universities about admission to a graduate program. However, I was unable to get accepted to graduate school before leaving Nigeria. I was more than a little disheartened. What was wrong with me that I could not get accepted to a graduate program? There had been no mention of this problem before, either by Dr. Proctor or Mr. Shriver. I had gotten answers to the three questions that Dr. Proctor had raised: I now knew some important people; I had traveled more of the world that I ever dreamed of; and I had $2000 in the bank, but I still couldn't get into a graduate school. When I tried to come back to America, there was nothing here to connect with, so I had to create a new plan.

Rest Stop: Switzerland

While serving in Nigeria, I made an acquaintance with a fellow Peace Corps volunteer by the name of Tom Morgan. Tom had graduated from Howard University; he was a great deal more sophisticated than I was. He said, "Rather than lamenting not being accepted to a graduate school or having employment, let's go hang out on the Left Bank in Paris. We can drink wine, have fun, look at the ladies and get away from all the conflict going on in America."

I said, "Tom, that is a great idea, let's go to Europe." We headed for Paris, but I never made it all the way. We stopped in Switzerland, and this stopover was destined to be one of the great marker events in my life. In Switzerland, we didn't have a rigid schedule. We found a place to live in Neuchatel; Neuchatel is French for "new castle"; it was a lovely little city on Lake Neuchatel.

One day, while Tom and I were sitting at a restaurant drinking wine, several tall men in sneakers came by. They said they were going to play a game of basketball. I had not played much basketball since leaving Tennessee State, though I did play a little while teaching the young Nigerians. I took the basketball from one of the men and began to dribble it between my legs. Though I was a little tipsy, out of practice and frustrated about not being able to get into graduate school, I still had an attraction to the round ball. I continued to bounce the ball between my legs like a member of the Harlem Globetrotters.

The guys watching said, "Mister, you are really a great ball handler." They ordered some wine and beer and we drank and laughed together. Then they asked, "We're going to play a game; are you interested in coming along?" I went with them; I already had on my basketball shoes. We went out to a little court and played for about two hours. At the end of the game I had scored thirty-three points. They asked me if I would like to play regularly on their team. Since I was only passing through Switzerland on my way to a leisurely stop in France, and was not in a great rush to leave, I said to them, "Why not?"

When Tom asked me what was going on, I told him that maybe I should stay in Switzerland a little longer. He said, "Man, the women in Paris are so much more beautiful than these in Switzerland; let's go!"

I said, "Tom, are we looking for what we are going to do with our lives, or are we looking for beautiful women?"

Tom amusingly said, "Beautiful women and wine, man!"

I said, "No, I think I'm going to stay here, play ball and see what develops."

Tom said, "I'll stay a couple of days, and then I'm headed for Paris."

Since we were in the French-speaking part of Switzerland, I decided that if I intended to spend more time there, I needed to learn French; and there was a university in Neuchâtel. I explained to Tom that I intended to enroll in a few classes and learn to speak French.

Tom agreed to stay for a couple of weeks while I was taking the French classes. One of us needed to speak the language, whether we remained in Switzerland or went to France. While I was taking my lessons, Tom met a young lady that he thought was interested in him. He took her to have a drink, a little fellowship and a nice time. Later, after he had piqued my interest, he said, "By the way, she's from America."

I also learned that this woman was a student living with a Swiss family for the summer term. Tom had met her and taken her out while I was busy with the basketball team. One afternoon after a game, he came back to our room and reported on his date. He said, "She is really nice, she's beautiful and extremely well mannered."

I said, "I hope you had a good time."

Again, he emphasized, "I don't know, Jerry, she's kind of strict, but if you are interested, I'll introduce you to her."

I said, "Tom, I want to play basketball, get myself in the groove, return to the states and get back to the Civil Rights Movement."

"I'll introduce her to you anyway," Tom responded. So, we went to meet her at the Café Neuchâtel.

When she arrived, Tom said, "Jerry, I'd like to introduce you to Muriel West." I greeted Muriel and in our conversation I learned that she was from Long Island, New York. She had graduated from Fisk University in 1966. I had received my bachelor's degree from Tennessee State, which was right down the street from Fisk, a couple of years earlier. I had never met a woman like her. I'd spent a lot of time with basketball players and other guys trying to talk to young ladies; I knew all the jokes about women, but I had never met a woman like this.

Here was a woman who had finished college with a foreign language major, and she was the most beautiful woman I had ever met. For her graduation gift, she chose to come to Switzerland for three months and live with a Swiss family so that she could perfect her French, as well as learn about another culture. She made it clear to me that she had no interest in getting involved with a boyfriend who was a basketball player.

Actually, I didn't want to get involved with a girlfriend either; I just wanted to have a little fun. My definition of having fun and Muriel's definition of having fun were not the same. What I wanted to do came from a strong drive found in most males. When she heard my desire, she said, "Maybe you need to look elsewhere for your fun." Instead of getting more deeply involved with me, she went back to America and began working for a company whose name I couldn't even pronounce – X E R O X. I stayed in Switzerland, playing basketball. While in Switzerland, I made money by transcribing tapes and playing basketball; I enjoyed the country and the Swiss people.

Return to the United States

After spending the better part of a year in Switzerland, I decided that it was time to return to the U.S. and continue to seek admission to a university where I could get a master's degree. I had applied to a number of colleges and universities, but I didn't get admitted to any of them. Since I was returning through the port of New York, I decided to visit with Muriel West; I made contact with her in hopes of visiting for a short time when I passed through New York. In the year that I remained in Switzerland, Muriel had begun working for Xerox as the first Black customer representative. She worked in uptown and downtown Manhattan, and was making quite a name for herself. She was, and is, a classy, intelligent lady.

Muriel had written to me that her parents were eager to meet me, but meeting them for the first time was a bit awkward and unnerving for me. Though they were very gracious to me, I was thrown off balance by their academic and professional achievements and middle class lifestyle. For example, they were traditional in the way they took their meals as a family and believed in the tradition of a suitor requesting the hand of their daughter in marriage, if an engagement was to take place. At mealtime they sat down to eat at an appointed hour; they spent time after the meal discussing the day and drinking tea; then they retired to the living room for more conversation. This was foreign to me, coming from a large family where everyone had varied eating schedules.

On this first visit in the West home, I got an idea of who they were. Her father was a brilliant chemist who had attended Lincoln University with the former president of Nigeria. Since I didn't come from a college family, meeting Mr. West created a sense of anxiety in me. Muriel's mother was a college graduate also. She had a Bachelor's and Master's degree in English from Fisk University. She and Mr. West met when they were teaching at Philander Smith College in Little Rock, Arkansas. Not too long afterward they married and remained in Arkansas where they continued teaching.

From there her parents moved to New York where Mr. West went to work in a medical laboratory. He was a chemist and a bacteriologist and used this knowledge to great personal advantage. After a few years of working for a salary, he started his own medical laboratory and was the first Black man in New York to own a medical laboratory. Neither my mother nor my father had been to college, and my father's ministry was confined to small churches with low pay. It was understandable that Muriel's parents were interested in learning more about me.

As I dealt with my insecurity, Muriel kept telling me that her parents were really down to earth people, that they completely accepted me. Even with Muriel's reassurance, I still felt ill at ease with her parents, and I didn't handle my feelings very well. In the few days that I visited their home, I learned about all I could manage. The Wests were great people, but so different from those I had grown up with; I loved them dearly. I soon departed for Gary, Indiana where I had an aunt and a cousin, Stella Mae Woods. My cousin was kind enough to invite me to live in her house while I was looking for a job.

In Gary, Indiana I found myself again in the middle of the Civil Rights Movement led by Mayor Richard Hatcher. He was born in Michigan City, Indiana, received a B.S. degree in business and government from Indiana University; and a bachelor of law with honors in criminal law from Valparaiso University School of Law in 1959. He moved to Gary and began practicing law in East Chicago, Indiana. In Gary, Indiana's history Richard Hatcher was the first and only freshman elected president of the City Council. He was also the first elected Black mayor of a U.S. metropolitan city, an office he held for twenty years.

While living with my cousin, I was working at the steel mill in Gary to earn a living, as well as serving tables on the railroad. Simultaneously, I was trying to get accepted into Northern Illinois University. During this time, Muriel and I wrote to each other and sometimes talked on the telephone; this was long before the day of cell phones and unlimited calling. I was challenged with the question of how I could impress and marry Muriel. Although we were apart, I was falling more and more in love with her each day.

On another visit to New York, I witnessed the commitment that Muriel's father and mother had to their community. They seemed to have always been people who worked in the community. They lived in the heart of the community and never considered moving out to the suburbs. They so treasured their inner-city neighborhood that they stayed and worked to better it. Muriel's parents worked hard to establish a community center, which became the center of life in the neighborhood.

Inspired by Muriel's parents, domestic workers from other parts of the country came to Hempstead and were trained to get good jobs in homes all around Hempstead. The community center provided a place for the workers to go when they left Long Island, the place of their employment, at the end of the day. The community center became something like a YWCA for them, except on a much smaller scale. Organizations like the Girl Scouts, Brownie Scouts and the Boy Scouts used the center.

Mr. West became the chairman of the housing authority; the housing project was just across the street from their home. He also took care of the young men and organized the professionals of the neighborhood. He was a Republican who followed the leadership of the party that Abraham Lincoln inspired. He was certainly an inspiring man.

Our letters and phone conversations inspired another visit to see Muriel and her family. I knew that when I got to her home I would get another dose of culture. Something happened the first day of my visit that could have completely ruined my chances with Muriel. In years since, we have referred to it as "the brown bag" incident. Though I had gotten to know Muriel's parents much better, out of respect I still did not feel free to drink wine in their presence. On this trip, I brought myself a little bottle of wine and walked across the street to the park where I met some guys to shoot some hoops. Occasionally, we paused and took a sip of the wine I brought. I was thinking that at about 6:00 p.m. I would slip back across the street for dinner. In the meantime, I was playing basketball and sipping wine. I had to finish the whole bottle because I had spent sixty cents to buy it and I wasn't planning to waste any.

There was a reason why I felt like I had to go over to the park to have a drink of wine. I was raised in the home of a preacher who thought it was a sin to smoke, drink or swear, and I thought her parents probably felt the same way. I would never have taken a drink in my father's house. Muriel and her family were Episcopalians, and they had wine in communion and at other times as well. They might have even had brandy. So given my background, I would not disrespect their home. I surely didn't want them to think of me as a drunk, because they wouldn't want their daughter to marry a guy addicted to booze.

Eventually, Muriel came out and said, "Dinner is ready."

I didn't pay any attention to her.

After a few moments she said. "Jerry, dinner is ready." And she turned to walk toward the house. I decided it was time for me to follow.

"It's time to eat," she said.

I came inside from the park and sat down at the table.

Mrs. West said, "Have you washed your hands?"

Without saying a word, I got up, went to the bathroom, washed my hands, came back and sat down again.

A minute later, Mr. West said, "How are you, Jerry?"

With obvious annoyance I said, "I'm fine!" I will admit that I had a little attitude problem.

What had bothered me most that evening pertained to the wine. You see, when Muriel abruptly called me to dinner, I hid the wine under some leaves in the park and when I went back to get it, somebody had stolen my wine. Plus, when her mother politely asked if I had washed my hands, I thought she was putting me down.

When everyone was seated at the table, Mrs. West served all the plates and passed them around. On the plate was lamb with green mint jelly. I wasn't familiar with mint jelly, so I assumed that we needed a biscuit for it. I learned that night that we didn't. Following the conversation about the lamb and green jelly, I asked to take their daughter out and they obliged. I thought going out was a simple matter – get up, put on a sweater, go out to the car and leave. But no! It wasn't that way in the West home. There was protocol. Before we left, Mr. West said, "If you are taking my daughter out, you need to have a necktie." Immediately I noticed Muriel's mother standing there with a necktie in hand. Mrs. West was always smooth and reassuring. She said, "If you don't have a necktie, here is one for you." I put the tie on for their sake, but as soon as I got in the car, I ripped it off. I just didn't like feeling manipulated.

Though we had never been to the place before, after just a few minutes' drive, we arrived at Fuzzy's Nightclub. Fuzzy's was just a hole in the wall, but we didn't realize that it was so modest until we got inside. When we walked in, the noise and smoke gave us a rude welcome, but soon we got into the rhythm of the music and I had a few drinks. I must confess, I had a ball. Everywhere I looked, I saw boys and girls drinking, singing and having fun. The next day when Mr. and Mrs. West asked, "How did you enjoy the evening?" I said, "It was fantastic!"

After visiting Muriel, I went back to Gary where I was working in the steel mills and waiting tables on the train. I had been able to save a little money, and I was feeling more confident that I would get into Northern Illinois. I called Muriel and said to her, "I've been thinking about it. I've saved up enough money to buy a new Chevrolet Camaro; the note is sixty-seven dollars a month, and I want to get married." It was just a matter of fact with me – working in the mill, saving my money, trying to get into Northern Illinois University, buying a car and getting married. Muriel felt that my proposal was a little premature. She had a great job in Manhattan and was not ready to get married.

Muriel said, "I love you, but I'm not ready to get married right now." After that response from her, I hung up the phone. I was angry. How could she turn me down? She had rejected my proposal. Even if it was premature and over the phone, it was genuine. I vowed that I'd never call her again. For several weeks tension mounted between us, mainly because of my stupidity. I stewed inside, "If that's the way she wants to be, it's no sweat off me." After a few weeks, Muriel called to speak with Stella, my cousin. Later on, in my presence, Muriel admitted that she initiated that call to my cousin with a different motive in mind. She wanted to marry me, but the time was not right for her. Perhaps I also needed some time. She had never met my family or been to my house. And as I've learned over the years, she is usually very sound in her decision making.

When I asked, Muriel explained to me why she rejected my original proposal like this: "I needed more commitment than you had offered, because marriage was not a temporary thing for me. I was marrying you for better or for worse, for the rest of our lives. If we're marrying, it is for life. It's not trying it out to see if it works. I had to meet your parents and other members of your family." Sound counsel then, even sounder today.

So, Muriel came to Gary and met my cousin, my aunt and some of their friends. Everybody fell in love with Muriel. Then we went to see my mother and father and my little sister, Tony. All of my relatives thought that Muriel was wonderful, which was no surprise to me. She captivated them with her style and grace, a gift she has used all of our married life.

But then the time came for me to talk to her parents about my intentions. The next time I visited Muriel, Mrs. West said, "You need to ask her father for her hand in marriage." Once again, I was a little insulted that I had to ask him to marry her, but I accepted the fact that they were a traditional family and this was the way traditional families did it. You asked the father for his daughter's hand. I didn't want just her hand, I wanted all of her. But her mother insisted that the appropriate thing to do was to ask her father for her hand in marriage, so I did.

I went into the living room, where her father was reading the newspaper, and sat down in a big comfortable chair. After a few minutes Mr. West said, "Jerry, what are you thinking about?" He always seemed to appreciate any idea that I had in my head. He would always listen to my ideas, elaborate on them and ask questions. He had many ideas too, and sometimes we enjoyed sharing our dreams with one another.

Little did I know, Mr. West always had a little Scotch in the cabinet. We began to sip a little Scotch and share our thoughts.

I'd been sitting with him for a few minutes when he said, "Jerry, you appear to have something on your mind. Tell me about it." He was so perceptive.

I said, "No, Mr. West, there is nothing on my mind." Finally, I gathered up my courage, looked him in the eye, and said, "Mr. West, I love your daughter, and I'd like to marry her. I'm asking you for her hand in marriage."

He said, "Well, Jerry, I think you are a very nice person and I'm thankful you asked me. Sure, I'm happy to offer you Muriel's hand in marriage." We got married on August 17, 1968. We were married in Hempstead, New York by an Episcopal priest at St. John's Episcopal Church. In 1967, the prior year, I had been accepted into Northern Illinois University.

My future was unfolding before my very eyes!

God never sleeps. He doesn't even nod. He sees and knows every thought and deed. That's frightening!!!

CHAPTER FIVE

✪

I Am Amazed at the Hand of Providence

THROUGHOUT MY PEACE CORPS tour of duty and even while I was in Switzerland playing ball and transcribing and translating documents, I was writing to universities trying to get into graduate school. The admissions office at Northern Illinois University in DeKalb, Illinois responded positively to my request and admitted me to a Master's program in Community Mental Health. Dr. Marvin Powell headed that department. When I shared with Dr. Powell the number of colleges and universities to which I had applied and been turned down, he said, "Perhaps one of the reasons that you were denied admittance was that you were being seen as a potential troublemaker, despite the fact that you are bright and intelligent." When I applied to those institutions, the admissions committee likely had been warned about admitting me because I had been deeply involved with the Civil Rights Movement and thus would possibly incite students to get involved. That day I promised Dr. Powell that I would study hard, discipline my behavior and earn my degree. The truth about how others perceive you sometimes hurts, but it also helps and heals.

Three weeks after I entered Northern Illinois University, a group of undergraduate students came to me, an "old man" of 26 years, with a challenging request. The students had come to NIU from the poor sections of Chicago, and they relayed feelings of personal rejection and verbal abuse. They said to me, quite frankly, "This university is not responsive to the needs of Black students." I was a Black graduate student and felt all was well—granted, I was older. I had also promised

Dr. Powell that I would not incite others to "stand their ground."

I believe the students targeted me because they thought that I was aligned with the administration. They dug even deeper and asked me about my role at the university. I said to them, "I'm going to keep my nose clean and finish this degree; I'm not going to lose my Fellowship." I had promised Dr. Powell that I would not cause any problems, yet these students were accusing me of being an "Uncle Tom". They assaulted me with this question, "Why don't you do more for the cause of Black people?" They didn't realize that in the 60's I was at the heart of the Civil Rights Movement in Nashville. They really didn't care what I had done in the past; they wanted me to speak up for them now in the midst of their pain. In response to their concern and with the counsel of my advisor, Dr. Powell, we founded the AACO – African-American Cultural Organization. This group could act as a sovereign body to negotiate agreements with the administrators of the university and help us attract other inner-city students to Northern Illinois. I also struggled with the question of how to harmonize these various demands being put on me, all while being a new husband. I was enrolled in a demanding program, living with a new, young bride and contemplating becoming involved, yet again, in the Civil Rights Movement. I was committed to my degree program and wanted to excel.

For a number of years, the university had received funding from the federal government for a counseling program that looked at the mental health deficiencies in the community. When the government began to analyze this expenditure, they recognized that more than counseling was needed; there were issues of mental health throughout the community that needed attention. As a consequence the government instituted the Community Mental Health Program. In some ways, there was a correlation between this program and the work that I did in Nigeria, helping communities to become more holistic and sensitive to the needs of all the residents. Under Dr. Powell's tutelage I was getting a master's in psychology and community mental health and since this program at Northern Illinois focused on helping individuals from a psychological point of view, I was discovering that it was the perfect program for me. I began to understand the conflicts and concerns of the community. As a result of this work, my master's thesis dealt with procedures for bringing communities together. This required developing methods to locate the gatekeepers and the power brokers and involve them as agents of change. My internship for the Community Mental Health Program was in Rockford, Illinois at the Singer Zone Center. I was assigned as an intern to this center for mentally challenged people.

One night I was playing table tennis at the center with a guy who seemed fairly normal. As we played, I said something about beating him. At first, he started laughing and joking, but then he walked around the table, grabbed me by the throat, and nearly broke my neck. I was unaware that my comments about beating him at table tennis would trigger deep-seated personal emotions that he could not control. He was promptly placed in a strait jacket. I learned later that this man was at the center because he attempted to kill his children when he thought that they were putting him down. This encounter caused me to question whether this was the right internship for me.

Student Riots and Demands

In addition to completing my internship and my thesis, I was also serving as the Director of the CHANCE Program at Northern Illinois. During my tenure, the students that belonged to the AAOC came to me with what they called "non-negotiable" demands that they wanted me to present to the administration. Their concerns were around African-American admissions criteria, additional African-American teachers and a stronger Afro-centric curriculum. In their protest, they also included their desire to have a more soulful variety of foods in the cafeteria, foods which reflected African- American cuisine. Among their demands was also a request for different living arrangements. In the 1960's these same demands were erupting in colleges and universities across the country. African-American students wanted these institutions to be more sensitive to their educational, psychological, and social concerns.

As the representative for Black students, I took all these concerns to the Chancellor of the university. These student demands were just beginning, and universities had not yet exploded with student riots, but there were definite signs of unrest. The demands we were facing at Northern Illinois were also surfacing on other campuses in Illinois, like the University of Illinois in Urbana-Champaign and Northwestern University in Evanston. Numerous universities across the country were facing the demands for student recognition and involvement in decision-making as students reflected on their lives as Africa- Americans in a predominantly white environment. Various groups of protestors were occupying buildings, chaining doors to buildings and making non-negotiable demands of all sorts. These protests came from student unrest created in part from feeling ignored, disrespected and treated as if they were unwanted and unwelcomed on campus.

I learned through these conflicts that problems create opportunities. As a result of the unrest demonstrated by student demands, we founded another organization called C H A N C E—Complete **H**elp and **A**ssistance **N**ecessary for a **C**ollege **E**ducation. We instituted this program with the assistance and blessing of the university. The CHANCE program created a positive method of access to the administration. With the success of our early efforts to create understanding and broaden the curriculum to include more diversity, the university allocated funds to support the program. Sharing in this endeavor with me were Deacon Davis and Bobby Sterns. The university funded salaries for the three of us to provide a place where minority students could feel a genuine sense of inclusion and involvement at the university. We subsequently encouraged the white students to become active with their fellow classmates in the CHANCE program. The university also made available a house on the university campus which we named the CHANCE Program House. We used this house to meet with the admissions office, the chairs of the various departments and the administrators of the university to plan strategies for successfully implementing the goals of the CHANCE program. We focused on recruiting and developing entrance and transitional strategies to keep students positively engaged. I had gone to Northern Illinois University to pursue a degree in Community Mental Health and, to my surprise, I was actively involved with the students, university, and DeKalb community in becoming a coalition. I faced the opportunity then, and those lessons are a part of who I am today.

As we sat around the table in the CHANCE program house, we sought methods to respond to the needs that we had uncovered through responding to student demands. Informed by the insights we had gained, we journeyed into the heart of Chicago and to the outlying areas around Chicago to recruit African-American students for the university. However, major issues with the faculty and admissions office confronted us. At the forefront of our concerns was how to alter the entry requirements and not change the requirements for graduation. Students who did not have adequate college preparation in high school often had serious problems gaining admittance. The rigorous demands for admittance into the university made it very difficult for students from inner city schools, who may not have adequately mastered the basics, to compete at the college level. Lack of adequate preparation, coupled with unfounded racist views in the university environment, hampered our efforts to get Black students enrolled.

Obviously, the faculty did not want to admit unprepared or poorly prepared students. So, we initiated conversation with the faculty and the administration about reviewing the entry requirements. We also questioned what could be done to better prepare the entering freshmen who needed extra assistance. Through CHANCE the university developed both a program and a style that made NIU the kind of university that achieved results. I am convinced more than ever that this open spirit of cooperation is still needed today. And when I review the results of the work that was done in 1968, one name above all others comes to my mind: President Rhoten A. Smith of Northern Illinois University. Dr. Smith should go down in history as an administrator who was unafraid to challenge the *status quo* in higher education. Because of this man and others like him across America, the higher education system began to be more inclusive of students of diverse backgrounds, color and economic status. The work of these pioneers created an emerging racial constituency in American universities. Their work has changed our expectations of who attends college, how they are evaluated and how they are encouraged as graduates. No longer are we shocked when we see a Black quarterback at the University of Alabama or the University of Florida. Today we recognize and accept these men just as we recognize other students who have succeeded in their respective colleges and vocations. No longer is it unusual to see successful Black entrepreneurs, professionals, entertainers and athletes. Accessibility and a level playing field, with equal opportunities, produce a stronger, diverse nation.

As could be expected, clashes developed between white professors and African-American students; the students felt that the professors did not understand them, their life experience and what they required to exist in a totally different environment. This lack of understanding by the university led to our bringing professionals to the campus to help and speak with Black students. Our goal was to counsel the students and to influence the professors who lacked experience with African-Americans. These meetings could at times be tense, but the tension was a necessary component of creating understanding. Communication is absolutely essential for racial progress. There must be mutual respect and trust if understanding is to prevail.

Fred Hampton

One of the persons we invited to visit the campus at Northern Illinois was Fred Hampton, who originally led the youth movement of the NAACP in Chicago. He left the NAACP because of his frustration with red tape and became the leader of the Black Panther Party in Chicago. The theme of the Black Panther Party was: "We will get our freedom and equality by any means necessary." His intense concern matched my own, and we were willing to go to any lengths to get equality and parity for students on the campus. "By any means necessary" could mean picketing, locking down buildings, and every other non-violent means of influencing change. We held press conferences and marched in protest – whatever was necessary.

In the late 60's the movement had come to the conviction that we would stand our ground, whatever that required. The use of any means, with no limit to where it might take us, caused a conflict for me. I had been strongly influenced by Dr. King and his emphasis on non-violence. My non-violent approach at times put me in direct conflict with some of the other the students. Often the students did not understand my reluctance to turn to violence; they sometimes criticized me, claiming that I resisted violence because I was paid by the administration to do the administration's will. They saw my actions as supporting their enslavement and bondage. It takes courage to prevail when the odds are seemingly stacked against you.

Fred Hampton spoke at the campus one night and fired up all the students to continue to demand changes. The administration and the police stayed away from the meeting, and we were able to keep the peace on campus that night. Two days later, Fred Hampton was murdered, along with others in his home, by the Chicago Police Department.

The Chicago police went into Fred Hampton's house and killed him and his family. Mark Clark, an associate, was also killed. The first reports stated that Hampton and Clark had opened fire on the police, but that was not true. Fred was found shot to death in his bed. The FBI, the Cook County Sheriff and the Chicago police conspired to murder Fred Hampton. I was on the campus when I learned that he had been killed. I was stunned and so were all the students who turned to me for an explanation. I had to make a fast decision, one that was as forthright as possible. My decision was that we maintain our non-violent stance on campus. Fred had encouraged us to get involved in the struggle, and now Fred was dead. We met, we screamed, we cried out for justice; we didn't understand why this murder had occurred. We all felt confused, disorganized and depressed with what had happened before our very eyes. With Fred's death, dialogue between faculty and students began on the campus in earnest. The faculty and the administration began to take more seriously the demands of the students, and developed a willingness to sit down and talk through their differences. As a consequence of discussing the issues openly, today the graduates of the program are spread throughout the country making positive contributions in their circles of influence. At the time, I did not realize that all the experiences I was having at Northern Illinois were preparing me for the next big challenge of my life.

The U.S. Office of Education

Dr. Don Bigelow headed the Office of Career Opportunities in Washington, D.C. He had heard that there was a young man who was standing up to injustice at Northern Illinois University. He contacted me and inquired if I would take a job with the United States Office of Education in Washington, D.C. I accepted the job with the Office of Education and was given a pay grade of 13, a very high rating for a young man working in Civil Service. When Dr. Bigelow hired me, he asked me to assist in managing the Career Opportunities Program. In many ways this was an enhancement and expansion of the work that I had done as Director of the CHANCE Program at Northern Illinois University. The task focused on curriculum development, assessing college entrance requirements for students without a strong GPA, part-time students and students who had to remain on the job because they could not stop working to become full-time students. These young men and women from the urban area needed an education too, if they were to advance up the economic and vocational ladder of American society.

I was placed under Dr. Wilton Anderson, a very powerful Black man who had graduated from Harvard University; I received his tutelage and he became my coach and mentor. He talked with me encouragingly about developing career opportunities for the disenfranchised and the marginalized people all over America, particularly in the inner city. He had a constructive vision for the role of marginal and vocationally frozen people in America. He sent me into various sections of the country to help design and set up career ladder programs, which provided a step-by-step way for marginalized people to get into the mainstream economic structure in America.

My passion also was to find a way to enable marginalized people to move up in the areas of job responsibility and pay grade in various American companies. As a result of the push for Equal Employment Opportunity (EEO) for all citizens, greater education for minorities became essential. There was pressure to hire minorities, but they were primarily confined to the most menial jobs with little hope for upward mobility. Our job was to help employers see how they could educate and develop minority groups into valuable employees. We wanted them to understand that additional education would enable them to serve their company more effectively. Another thing I emphasized to these employers was that if they gave these young people access and opportunity, they would be assured greater productivity.

While I was working in the Career Opportunities Program in the Office of Education, I was introduced to Dr. Elias Blake, Jr. and Dr. Frederick S. Humphries. They worked for a company called The Institute for Services to Education Inc. I resigned from the federal government to work for ISE. This company was funded with Title III money. Title III money was government-appropriated funds that were made available to minority colleges and universities. The educational institutions used these funds to employ ISE to assist them in developing curriculum for students who needed assistance with college-level work and for students who desired to explore inter-disciplinary studies. I was very familiar with these issues. The educational institutions, colleges and universities contracted with ISE to develop faculty, curriculum, and administrative plans for the school as well as techniques for fund development initiatives. We worked primarily with historically Black colleges to enable them to acquire the skills that would enhance their ability to compete with mainline institutions of higher education.

Every summer we invited representatives from thirty to forty historically Black colleges and universities to Boston, Massachusetts for six weeks. During this month-and-a-half we worked together to create the freshman curriculum, which would be taught in an inter-disciplinary fashion on their respective campuses. This manner of instruction was on the cutting edge of higher education. Our pedagogy was to integrate the various disciplines, so as to give each student the best opportunity to graduate from college with a well-rounded experience. If we used an inter-disciplinary approach to creating the curriculum, it required the inter-disciplinary teaching of the material. Our progress in this pedagogy rippled throughout the college ranks. ISE became a leading consulting firm creating curriculum and training material to teach from an inter-disciplinary, subject matter approach.

We were concerned with those students who lacked adequate

high school preparation, similar to the ones that I had worked with in Illinois. We were teaching teachers that if students are to learn how to live in a community, they needed to learn the integrated realities of the community. For the students to learn in an integrated way, the teachers had to teach in a collaborative manner. The math teacher was instructed to call attention to the use of proper grammar in math equations, and the history teacher was required to call attention to math concepts in history. Whatever the issues, it was important for the teachers to work in an integrated fashion to help the students become mature, well prepared and successful. Underlying this style of teaching was the necessity of every student having strong self-esteem – to feel self-worth, to have dignity, and to have a sense of personhood. Nothing is more important for an education than for marginalized persons to know who they are and like who they are.

A guy named Cliff Johnson from the University of New Orleans humorously illustrates this integrated way of teaching. He was a humanities teacher who loved music and jazz, and he liked to use imaginative, creative methods in his class.

One day Cliff said, "I can get with the biology teacher, and we can work out a curriculum to show that certain odors come from a man and from a woman that indicate to each that they are being attracted to one another." He reminded us that in Africa they did not wear deodorant because they needed to have free access to the odor that flowed from others' bodies. He said that humans experience sensory elements just like animals, which tell them the proper time to make approaches. He emphasized that these aromas come from the human body, which are not only physiological, but they also have psychological and social consequences. He wanted to do a play on "The Scent of a Man."

About this time, a new perfume came out called Musk. Cliff bought some Musk and brought it to the classroom for us to test. How did it affect a man? And, how did it affect a woman? The group had a divided opinion. Nevertheless, this experiment reveals both a daring spirit and the willingness of our group to experiment with new forms of learning.

As I have indicated, teachers were encouraged to emphasize that the number one asset a student could have was a positive view of one's self. No longer can we perpetuate a slave mentality because we are not slaves. Slavery is not part of our being; it is an act committed against us by others. How important it is to stop thinking about ourselves with a slave mentality! All of this boils down to one thing – helping every student to be a real human being, filled with self-worth and confidence that he or she can achieve something of value in the world. This revised point of view affects the whole life of people – the way they feel, the energy they have and their drive to accomplish dreams and visions.

We were created in a beautiful image – the image of God. When teachers began to see students differently – as persons of worth and great potential – the level of communication improved because of their positive attitude. When the teachers saw the students change and grow, they began to have more confidence in the program and in themselves and what they were seeking to achieve.

Concurrent with my work with the University of Massachusetts in these summer programs, at Dr. Wilton Anderson's suggestion I began work on a doctor's degree. I wondered how I could begin work on a doctorate when I had a full-time job in Washington D.C. I also had to support two small children and a wife. The administration at the University of Massachusetts put together a special program for persons like me who could not do residency for two or three years. My advisor gave me reading to do and papers to write; they made these assignments dovetail with the research and creative work I was doing on curricula for African-American colleges and universities. While I was consulting with those colleges and universities and spending six weeks with them each summer, plus visits to their campuses, I also was writing up projects, taking courses, and earning credit for an advanced degree.

While I was working on this curriculum, I also began writing my dissertation. My thesis was that young Black boys are treated differently from young Black girls and that this fact conditions later behavior. What a young Black girl does when she's six or seven years old does not define her. She will be told in warm, encouraging words that she should not do particular things. She is rarely put down, criticized or humiliated. On the other hand, when a young Black boy does a similar thing, he is firmly reprimanded and told to shut up, sit down, and that he must never do it again or else he will be beaten within an inch of his life. These two different styles of rearing children shape their idea of the world and their place in it. I demonstrated that more time with young males of six or seven would shape them for entry into the world beyond the family.

In order to gather information for my dissertation, I used the Aurora School System as the source of my data. When I had finished collecting data, I had more information than I knew what to do with. Some days I was pretty confused trying to figure out a way to organize the research and demonstrate my thesis.

My two advisors, Dr. Robert Suzuki and Dr. Cleo Abraham, were serious, even hard-nosed and demanding. It seemed to me that that they desired a certain amount of suffering in order to get a dissertation written and approved. I experienced a great deal of frustration. When I drove to Massachusetts for my summer work, I left Muriel with her parents in New York while I was writing my dissertation and being directed, scolded and encouraged by my advisors. There were days I wondered why I didn't just give up and go home.

One day an advisor said to me, "We want you to feel that you have really earned this degree; we don't want just anybody getting our degree without paying his dues."
And I will never forget how Dean Suzuki advised me, "Gerald, just go through it. Answer their questions. Don't try to know everything." I learned that day that being a smart aleck was not a good approach to completing a dissertation.

Before I left Dean Suzuki's office, he said, "Now I want you to write in your summary these words, 'there needs to be more work done in this area.'" But I responded that actually no more work does need to be done in this area. He said, "Yes, there does, and you'd better say it." My advisors said, "This is the process and whether you wish to go though it or not is your choice." I swallowed and did as I was advised.

Coincidentally, while I was working on my degree, I discovered there was another African-American man who had bought a house, paved an airstrip behind it and enrolled in a doctoral program in education at the University of Massachusetts. His name was Bill Cosby, and he was not too shabby company to keep. It took me four years to finish that degree and in the succeeding years, it has opened many doors for me to offer service in the field of education.

While I was writing about the background of my degree and the efforts I put forth to earn this degree, it occurred to me that I never told my parents I had a Ph.D. I wondered why I never told them. Would it have sounded boastful? Would they think that I felt superior to both of them? I would have liked for them to celebrate my success with me, so why would I not tell them? I really didn't know what to do, so I just kept it to myself. Of course they eventually found out, and all of my apprehensions were grossly without merit.

African-American Students and the Greater World

When African-Americans look back at the Fertile Crescent, the building of the pyramids, the creation of hieroglyphics and all of these early accomplishments, we tend to forget that they came from our ancestors. Our ancestors were creative, imaginative and productive. All African-Americans should know that they are somebody because their heritage is not one of slavery, but of humanness. No other group of people was brought to America in chains like our ancestors; they came under duress. Other groups from all over Europe, Israel and Asia freely chose to come to America, and some even paid their own way to get here. African-Americans are the only group of people that were enslaved and placed in chains for the trip. But we have had to rise above our gruesome history and are now our own persons living lives that contribute to the survival and success of others. We don't have to be ashamed of our dark pigmentation, our kinky hair or our wide noses. We can't afford to let people insult and put us down by bringing negative attention to stereotypical physical traits; we will not let ignorant name calling make us feel ashamed. We don't need to desire straight hair because our kinky hair keeps our scalps from burning in the sun. We don't concern ourselves with sunbathing, because we have a permanent God-given, beautiful tan. Brothers and sisters with big hips and big behinds should not be mocked because of their powerful physiques, but embraced and admired for their beauty. We must turn all of these perceived negatives into positives.

And despite our struggles with society, some continue to ask whether there is still a need and a place for historically Black colleges and universities. No matter what the University of Georgia or Georgia Tech or Georgia State may be able to teach African-American students, they still do not have the sensitivity that Black teachers have for the same students in a Black college or university. Basically, they do not understand the cultural influences that have shaped these students, and they misinterpret the world from which these students come and the environment that they will be going into after graduation. The world needs students like those who go to historically Black colleges and universities and express their gifts in business, law, banking and science. These scholars will bring different insights into their respective fields and the world. So without question, there is a place for Black colleges and universities where Black teachers teach Black students how to live in a growing, diverse culture. This diversity can uncover rare and necessary gifts that can come from no other sector of our society.

As I completed my dissertation, I began to look for my next challenge. And I soon found that when you complete a major milestone in life, God's divine guidance begins a new chapter.

CHAPTER SIX

✪

I Am Amazed at My Spiritual Awakening

I HAD MOVED FROM A DIRECTOR of African-American Students position at Northern Illinois University, to being an associate in the Office of Education in the United States government. In this role, I had the opportunity to explore the Civil Rights Movement more deeply and to create a tangible response to the need for improving the curriculum at Black colleges and universities. In addition, this position made it possible for me to earn my doctorate degree. Not only was I advocating for the uneducated and the poorly educated, I was working on a creative program that offered an avenue of training that gave people hope and encouraged greater participation in the American Dream. All of this was highly satisfying to me. But, one never knows how the Providence of God will unfold. What I am about to write is a testimony to the indescribable work of the Creator that has brought to me an unanticipated source of fulfillment in my life.

I had worked in the government and with a charitable foundation for ten years; however, I knew that the time was drawing near for me to reassess my commitment and engagement in Washington, D.C. I realized that it had come time for me to leave. I was somewhat apprehensive because I had a wife, a son and a daughter. But, I had to make new decisions about my life because, although I enjoyed my work, I was beginning to burn out. I was tired. Here I was with a master's and doctorate degrees, not knowing what I needed to do. Something in me knew that my current lifestyle was ending, and that soon I would be making a drastic and significant change in my life and future.

Dr. Elias Blake and Dr. Fred Humphries were President and Vice-President respectively of ISE (The Institute for Services to Education). Dr. Blake left ISE to become President of then Clark College in Atlanta, Georgia. Dr. Humphries had already been named President of Tennessee State University. He had asked me if I wanted to come to Tennessee State with him, but that position did not pan out. I found myself in transition both in my emerging vocation and my religious faith development. I had worshipped in a church filled with people who loved God, but who felt that no one was going to heaven but them. I had never seriously studied my faith convictions, but now it was coming to the forefront in my mind. I also began to realize that traveling all over the country visiting universities and faculties was no way to treat my wife and my two children. After leaving ISE, I collected a small unemployment check every week to survive. In that time of transition when I was struggling to find my way, a verse of Scripture, Proverbs 3:6, came to my mind: "In all your ways acknowledge him, and he will direct your path."

Death Comes Near

While I was in this state of uncertainty, I kept trying to figure out what to do. One snowy night a man from Amway came to our home trying to lure us into his business; he came in and sat down with Muriel and me and showed us how we could get rich selling Amway. He promised that his plan would earn thousands of dollars for us each year. Muriel and I had two children, Hasan and Nia. Hasan had a medical issue which concerned us greatly; he was born jaundiced and frequently experienced high fevers and chills. Occasionally, he had convulsions when his fever reached a certain temperature. We kept tepid water in the tub upstairs so that if he had a fever, we could lay him down in the tub and splash water on him to cool his fever.

Hasan had one of those episodes the night that the representative from Amway came to talk with us. He had a high fever and a convulsion, which immediately demanded our attention. The visitor heard Hasan's scream just as Muriel and I did. As quickly as we could, we picked Hasan up, put him in the bathtub and splashed water all over him. The visitor, visibly shaken by the situation, asked if he could help us in any way.

We lived in Oxon Hill, on a hilly street in Maryland. Outside the snow was falling, and the hill was dangerously slippery. The Amway representative had a Volvo with a front-wheel drive. Because his car could make it through the sleet and snow, he offered to drive us to the hospital. The five of us – the driver, Nia, Hasan, Muriel and I – got in the car and headed for the hospital. We took Hasan to the emergency room, and the attendants immediately admitted him to the children's ward. The gracious Amway representative bade me good-by and went on home before the weather got worse. I sat down in the waiting room with Nia in my lap, anxiously awaiting news about Hasan. Eventually, the waiting room emptied, and Nia and I waited alone. Those very anxious minutes stretched into hours. Waiting teaches patience and brings deeper insight into a situation. I learned a lot about patience that night.

At two o'clock in the morning, we were still the only ones in the waiting room. To occupy my mind, I began thinking about the Civil Rights Movement, about Tennessee State University, about my time in Africa, and about my time in higher education – all of these thoughts were running through my head uncontrollably. Since I had been raised in the church, I had an understanding of God's power. Though I did not believe the kind of dogmatic spiritual expressions that I had learned, they still had a spiritual influence and impact on me. During this crisis, my mind turned to who and what I believed God to be. I prayed, "God, if you can do anything, please help us!" I then began to make promises to God, bargaining with God, that I would do whatever He requested of me, if He would only save my son's life. In that struggle, I realized a poignant truth: God may not change the situation, but God can change the person. I know this to be true because God changed me from a man seeking his own will, to a man praying "let your will be done."

At this point in my prayer and weariness, I was only semi-conscious when I recognized a nurse getting off the elevator and heading straight toward me. With a great deal of feeling she said, "I regret to tell you that your son passed about two o'clock this morning, and your wife is up there with him now."

I looked up at her and said, "Thank you so much. I know what I need to do now; I can accept it. If this loss has come to me, God will help me through it."

The nurse responded immediately, saying, "I'm a Christian woman and I've never seen anyone have this kind of strong faith." Then she said, "Mr. Jones, you are a powerful man."

I looked at her, confused, and said, "My name is Durley, not Jones."

She said, "They told me upstairs that I could find Mr. Jones in the waiting room." "No, I'm the only one here and I'm taking care of my daughter, Nia, while her mother is with Hasan."

She said, "Let me go and check on your son's condition. I'll be back in a moment."

That moment seemed like an eternity. I watched her walk away, step into the elevator and then the door closed. I couldn't imagine what had happened to my son, and I honestly didn't know what had happened to me, except that I had gone into a different state of mind that was very peaceful and calm. I was sitting quietly, peacefully waiting to find out what God intended for me. As I was waiting, I heard the bell ding; the elevator door opened and out walked the nurse who had gone to check on Hasan. I sat calmly and showed no emotion.

She walked over to the couch where I was sitting, holding Nia. When I looked up at her, I knew in that moment that everything was okay. She delivered the news to me, "Mr. Durley, your son's fever broke two or three hours ago. I think he's going to be fine. Your wife will be down soon." After the nurse gave me that relieving report, she turned and walked back to the elevator. Though she had reported that he was fine, I wondered if Hasan had died and returned to life again. The power of prayer and the ultimate acceptance of God's will in your life are transformative.

The nurse had not been gone too long before Muriel came into the waiting room. There comes a time in all our lives when the best thing to do is to just be silent. Muriel sat there in silence as we both let the truth of our situation sink into our souls. We looked at each other, but neither of us said a word for some time. As we looked outside, the sun was just coming up. We both felt like we had lived an eternity in one night. Being the activist that I was, I asked Muriel, "What do we do now?" Though I had asked her an important, heartfelt question, she continued to stare into space, remaining in resolute silence. She was seemingly reflecting on all that had happened during the night and the miracle that had been granted to us. It's important to take time to experience and truly digest the countless miracles that God grants each of us daily.

When I finally spoke, I said, "I had a talk with God last night." I tried to explain to her what I had said to God about accepting whatever was to happen. She looked at me with an expression on her face that sent me a message: "Okay, that's fine." She seemed to be saying, "I've heard you say life-changing things like this before; now I'm wondering how long this will last." I have and will always love Muriel's pure, honest countenance which keeps me grounded. I truly love that woman.

"My mama used to say 'actions speak louder than words,'" I responded. That morning I promised Muriel that she would see a change in my life, but I pleaded with her to be patient with me. I knew that God had not finished molding me yet. Honestly, I didn't know exactly what I was talking about, but the words seemed to keep falling out of my mouth. In retrospect, those words turned out to be unbridled prophecy. Maybe I didn't know what I was saying; maybe she was right about the promises I'd made before. Or, perhaps I was just speaking to break the silence, but I believed that something really new and transformative had happened in me. I was excited to see the direction in which God was preparing to send me.

In this suspended spiritual state, I experienced no fear of surrendering to the unknown, because deep down inside I believed something good was happening to and for me. Normally, when a person is accustomed to being in charge and making things happen, like pulling people together, evaluating complex situations and devising successful plans, it is very uncomfortable to not know how all the pieces of life will eventually fit together. I knew those uncomfortable feelings, but this time was different: I was at peace; I knew that I had been touched by God, and my life was about to take an entirely new and different turn. Muriel and I looked at each other, and then at Nia, who was still asleep in my lap, and we hugged each other as we had never hugged before. We both said, "We'll see how it goes." There was no illustrative God talk; no utterances of Jesus told me this or that, no shallow clichés that we'd heard all of our lives. Some people might have said, "Nothing happens to you that you cannot find a way through." We made none of those responses. Both Muriel and I said, "We'll just wait and see how it turns out." When you get to that point, a certain kind of calmness and serenity, accompanied by true joy, covers your entire being. When you reach that point, it is easy to smile, laugh and accept your burdens. When this joy came to us out of the darkness of the night, I asked her if she wanted to plunge into this new life. She asked me, "What are you crying about?" There were tears of joy, tears of sadness, tears of redemption, and still we had no direction for our future, but we knew we had reached a new level of commitment and expectation – a spiritual level that we believed could carry us through any and every situation that would confront us. We believe that to this day. There is nothing that we, with God, can't handle.

I hailed a taxi to take us home because the Amway salesman who had brought us to the hospital had left hours before. Though the sun had come out earlier, it had begun to snow and the light of day darkened. I got in the taxi, and we went home together. When we got home, I really started feeling good and wanted to celebrate what had happened to Hasan, and to all of us. For years, one of the ways that I celebrated the good things in my life was to buy a bottle of Jack Daniels. Seemingly, sipping Jack Daniels and listening to good music always raised my spirits even higher. At the time, I owned a Chevrolet Camaro with an eight-track player; so I got in the car, cranked it up and went to the liquor store. I got a half-pint of Black Jack Daniels, just a half-pint, because I didn't want to drink too much. Then, I drove around town slowly in the snow, drinking Jack Daniels and listening to my eight-track. The idea struck me that I should have several drinks, as a libation, thanking God for bringing my son through. I rationalized my reasons to drink more. I thought, "What a fantastic day. A son who would live, a bottle of Jack Daniels and good music."

I said to myself, "I'm going up to Howard University, park my car, get out and go into the Rankin Chapel and thank God for what He's done for me." But I had only bought a half-pint of Jack Daniels, and I couldn't afford to run out, so I bought another half-pint to ensure that I had the proper "libation". I finally got to campus, parked my car and trudged over to Rankin Chapel. I tried to get into the chapel to pray and thank God for my blessings and my new commitment to serve Him. When I got to the door of the chapel, I found it locked. By this time I'd had a few more sips of Black Jack. I began banging on the door and shouting, "Let me in, let me in! I want to thank God for what He has done for me." God didn't stop me from getting inside the chapel; the campus police did. The campus policeman who apprehended me said, "Why are you trying to break into Rankin Chapel?" He then told me that he was taking me to the office of the campus police, where I would be charged with attempted breaking and entering, disturbing the peace, and damaging university property.

When we got to the office of the campus police, the policeman sat me in a chair and told me that he was calling the Washington, D.C. police to come and arrest me. He said, "You will be detained here until the D.C. police come." To make sure that I didn't run away, he put a pair of handcuffs on my wrists and cuffed me to the chair. I think he handcuffed me to the chair because he was suspicious of my story about wanting to speak to God and thank Him for saving my son. Perhaps the strong smell of Jack on my breath supported his suspicions. My banging on the door suggested to him that I was rowdy, rather than religious. Both of us were nice guys: I was loud and boisterous trying to get my own way, and he was kind and patient in doing his job. We waited and waited, but as you can imagine, the D.C. police had more important things to do on a snowy day than clean up a campus intrusion. What is a little rowdiness on a campus when a city like Washington, D.C. is overloaded with traffic jams, wrecks and violence that demand attention? Thank God that they were busy assisting others.

Several hours passed and I began to think a little more clearly as the cobwebs of Jack Daniels were flushed out of my brain. Some might say that I was sobering up. When a new guard came on duty, I said to him, "I am not a bad person; I may have had one drink too many, but I have both a master's and doctor's degrees. I've been working with Black colleges; I'm really not a drunk or a rowdy man. Can you forgive me this time, let me go and I promise that you, nor anyone else, will ever see me in this condition again."

He turned on the light, took the handcuffs off and we began to talk. At about five o'clock, when dawn was approaching, he said, "Why don't you go home now; you seem to be okay." I thanked him and walked out, relieved that I was not in a Washington, D.C. jail. It had been snowing and I couldn't remember where I parked my car. When I looked everywhere and couldn't find it, I decided that I needed to get my head straight and eat something. I went across the street to McDonald's, got some orange juice and sat down. When I opened my eyes, behold...there was my car parked right in front of McDonald's, exactly where I had left it when I made my pilgrimage to Rankin Chapel. I went outside, swept away the snow and eased out of the parking lot.

After finding my car, I should have gone home, but being a determined person, I still wanted to thank God for healing my son. The security officer who had released me said that Howard School of Divinity was up the street at the corner of Fourteenth Street and Randolph Street. So, rather than go home, I drove up the hill toward the Divinity School. On the way, I got stuck in the snow right in front of the School of Divinity. It was getting light and I was getting cold, when I heard a knock on the window of my car. I looked up and there was a light-skinned Black man asking, "Are you okay?" I looked at him and thought he was an angel sent to rescue me. Again, he asked, "Are you all right, are you all right in there? Come on inside and warm up." So I went into the man's office at the Howard Divinity School. It so happened that the man who rescued me was the Dean of the Divinity School, Dr. Lawrence Neil Jones, a UCC minister who I thought was doing part-time duty as an angel of mercy. At that time, I did not know that Dean Jones had been the Dean at Fisk when Dr. Martin Luther King came to Fisk University to promote the movement. He was the consummate human embodiment of who Christ called all of us to be.

The Dean and I began to talk, and I told him the story of my son, his healing, taking him home, driving downtown, drinking too much Jack and being arrested by the campus police. When I told my story, he fell out laughing. He laughed and laughed and said to me that maybe I needed to come to the Divinity School and find out what God is preparing me to do. It challenged me in that instant to seek God's will for my life.

I said to Dr. Jones, "I've had enough of God to take me through the rest of my life. I grew up on dysfunctional religious thinking, and I don't seek religion to find answers anymore."
He said, "Fine, you can muddle through in your own way trying to find out what God is doing with you, and you will find yourself in this same place at the end of your search."

I was insulted. I felt that the Dean was putting me down. I said to him, "I've got to leave; I've got to get out of here." I forgot that I was stuck in the snow and needed help to get out. Knowing my predicament, he took out his AAA card and called for help. The people at AAA came shortly and got me out of the slick, packed snow and into the street. He looked at me one last time and said, "See, God uses people to do His work. Come back and see me again." No one can do anything of any significance completely on their own. We all need God.

When I got home, I sat down with Muriel and told her the whole story. I told her about my experience with the Howard University police and about meeting Dr. Jones, the Dean of the Howard Divinity School. She loved me deeply and was completely understanding of my situation. She looked at me in a way that told me exactly what she was thinking: I should have stayed home and should not have been riding around drinking whiskey. She said, "You should have been here, helping me to take care of these children." I did what any other man would have done, I started pouting. I didn't say too much for a couple of days; I guess you could say that we had an extended quiet time between us, real quiet. Quiet time between those in love can strengthen their relationship. Dr. Jones' words resurfaced in my mind: "God uses people to do his work."

Attending Howard Divinity School

A few days later, I reluctantly gave him a call and asked if we could talk. With a beautiful sense of humor, he asked me if I thought I could find Howard Divinity School again. I told him that I thought so, since my head didn't hurt today and that I was thinking much more clearly. I got in the car and drove down to the Divinity School; I found it easily and went in and sat down with Dean Jones to talk about taking a course or two. He asked me, "Why take two or three courses? If you take twelve credit hours, you are a full-time student and the cost will be minimal."

I said, "But I'm not working right now, and I don't have enough money to finance any schooling."

He said, "Go ahead and register; I believe that things will work out." He concluded with an admonition that I will never forget, "Trust God!"

Introspectively, I thought that was the most ridiculous statement I could think of, because all my life I had been trusting myself.
I went home and told Muriel, "I'm going to enroll in the Howard School of Divinity."

She said, "You know, Jerry, there are two types of men that I never wanted to marry: one is a doctor and the other is a preacher." At that moment I assured Muriel that I was not thinking about preaching. I explained to her that I only wanted to learn how to talk to God, how to listen to God and learn how God works through people. I had no intention of being a preacher. My assurance seemed to allay her fears, and truthfully, I did not go to the divinity school with the idea that I would pursue pastoral work as a vocation. But our plans are not God's plans, nor His thoughts our thoughts. God knows what He wants each of us to achieve and when. Learn to quietly and humbly surrender to that still small voice inside.

I personally and emphatically had no interest in pastoral ministry because I had seen the cruelty of people toward their preachers; I had seen how churches treated their First Ladies. Pastoring, in my judgment, was a thankless, demanding, non-appreciated job. And besides these negatives, preachers didn't make any money. So, I kept saying to Muriel not to worry about being a pastor's First Lady because I was not going into the ministry; I simply wanted to learn more about God and God's ways. So I enrolled in Howard's Divinity School and began taking evening courses. I was on fire with learning so much and eliminating so much spiritual baggage that I had been carrying with me over the years.

I was probably the only "uncalled" person in the school. Everyone in the class could tell exactly when they were called, how God snatched them by the nape of the neck and personally called them into preaching the gospel. They could tell about how God had taken away their taste for liquor and gambling. All the other students could tell hair-raising stories about God in their lives, but I had no similar story to tell. I could have said, "God saved my son, and I wound up drunk, stuck in the snow and the Dean rescued me." But I was sure that it was not wise for me to tell too much of my story to these called, fire-breathing saints. I doubted they could handle my testimony of being "uncalled".

Many of those young preachers passed me and asked, "How were you called?"

I responded, "I don't have a calling." They said, "Then how are you going to preach the gospel, if you didn't get the call?" So, I began to feel like I needed to create my story of being called. Feelings of inadequacy made me question whether I was doing what "I" wanted or what "God" wanted for my life.

At that point I began to understand the difference between "a calling" and "a compelling." I was "compelled" to let God use my training in education and all my experiences with people in Nigeria, Illinois and Washington, D.C. for His glory. I had a "compelling," not a "calling". I have met many preachers, both in the divinity school and since, who were filled with good words about a call, but they didn't seem compelled to make a difference in the world. I knew deep inside that I was being compelled to make a difference in life for as many people as possible. We must learn to let positive forces in our lives compel us to pursue our purpose for living.

Because of the compelling notion of what I wanted to do, it was imperative that I stay in school. To earn money to live on, I helped make the first film about historically Black colleges and universities. I also wrote grant proposals and through these part-time jobs, I earned enough money to take care of my family. While I was engaged in part-time work and school experience, I met a man named Bill Siphax, who was a wealthy businessman in Washington, D.C. and a member of the Mount Olive Baptist Church in Arlington, Virginia. He talked to me about making money; he talked to me about taking care of my family; he talked to me about putting the Christian faith at the core of everything I do. He seemed, to me, like he was obsessed with God. He initially got on my nerves with so much Jesus talk.

After we got to know each other very well, he invited me to Mount Olive Baptist Church. As much as I liked Bill, as much as he was mentoring me, I could not see myself ever going into a Baptist church, because they had instrumental music. They were loud and they did not follow the teachings of Jesus Christ as I had been taught. In his own Socratic teaching method, Bill Siphax asked me, "Who told you this about Jesus? Who said all Baptists are going to hell? We are all Christians. Why do Christians fight among themselves?" I had told Bill that I had been taught in a church where they believed that Jesus built his church upon a rock and that rock was Peter. Since Jesus built his church on the Rock, it was the Church of Christ. It wasn't built on the Baptist Rock, or the Lutheran Rock, or the Presbyterian Rock; it was built upon the Rock of Jesus Christ. I was taught that Jesus built his church on the Rock of Peter who was the one that made the confession, "You are the Christ, the Son of the living God." And because Peter recognized who Jesus was, Jesus founded His church and its name is the Church of Christ, not Mount Olive Baptist Church.

Bill responded very simply, "Just come and worship with us and see what ideas you get." Reluctantly, I asked Muriel to consider worshipping at the Mount Olive Baptist Church with our children. I felt something very strange as I moved among those people, something that was disconcerting to me. They reached out in love to us, but they were still Baptist. I saw them enjoying themselves in worship. After service, they went out to eat together; and they acted like Christians.

The minister of this church was Rev. Aaron B. Mackley. They called him "the preaching boy wonder". He began preaching when he was five years old. When I met him he was eighty-two. He'd been preaching seventy-seven years; and I thought I knew more than him because I had been to seminary. In the service, he let me read the Scripture. Sometimes I edited the text a little and he rebuked me, saying, "Shut up. I didn't tell you to interpret, but to merely read the Scripture. Read it, sit down, and shut up." While teaching me how to do the invocation, he said, "When I ask you to do the invocation, 'God's presence,' not your presence, is asked for, so ask for God's presence to dwell among us and then sit down and shut up."

As I began attending that church, Aaron B. Mackley showed me how to take an offering, how to do communion, how to preach the gospel, and, in addition, this man was unwittingly re-shaping my life and future ministry. I began to know that God can work through anyone who believes and obeys the Word. Because of his influence, I began to see that maybe Baptists, Methodists, Presbyterians and Lutherans were Christians too because of what Reverend Mackley taught me. I believe that as a result of his work with me, today I can preach about service to God in the synagogue as well as speak about meditation in an Episcopal Church. I can attend a Methodist or Lutheran Church and feel at home because of the inclusiveness that I learned from Reverend Mackley. I have derived great spiritual benefit from attending "Jumah," Friday prayers at a mosque: I can bow with them and pray with them and still remain faithful to my Christian traditions.

I continued attending the Mount Olive Church until I finished my degree at Howard Divinity School. I had learned much from Reverend Mackley while working with his congregation. I felt prepared for the next phase of my life. I was not employed at the time; I had no offers of a job and I was receiving no pay from the Mount Olive congregation, though I was working there every week. Dean Jones' exhortation to trust God for all you need was more real than ever before.

An Unexpected Move

One day I got a call from Dr. Elias Blake, Jr., who had become the president of Clark College in Atlanta, Georgia. He was the former president of ISE, where I was employed for many years. He invited me to speak to the faculty at the opening convocation at Clark College. I said, "Yes, I would love to speak to your faculty." Both Dr. Blake and I had been productively engaged with a number of Black colleges. After I finished speaking with Dr. Blake on the phone, I wondered if this conversation had anything to do with the next chapter of my life. Perhaps I would continue work in higher education, but I had been shown how to use my newly acquired skills in a different capacity.

When I came to Clark College to speak to the professors at the opening of school, I focused on the needs of young Black students. I endeavored to help each one of the faculty members see that every student needed to be adequately prepared to make a difference in the world. I illustrated my lecture with my own life experience. I talked about what it meant to me to attend Tennessee State University, how my life was challenged and changed by the Civil Rights Movement, and what it meant to me to go to Africa and work among those Third World farmers and help them achieve goals greater than they had ever set for themselves. I spoke about working with students at Northern Illinois University and engaging the faculties of other colleges and universities when I was associated with the ISE office in Washington. I used all of those experiences to show how we must integrate everything we have learned to impact the students' education. I emphasized our responsibility to help them become mature, self-assured, successful individuals as they move out into the world. After I made this presentation to the faculty, Dr. Blake asked me if I could stay around a little while and continue to work with the faculty on an ad hoc basis. Following my presentation to the faculty, he gave me $300; I put $50 in my pocket and sent the rest to Muriel in Washington so she would have money for the family.

I remained in Atlanta primarily because President Blake desired more time to talk about issues that had come up in his personal life and exciting challenges that he was facing in his administration of the school. I actually slept in his house for a few days, and during that time he shared with me some of his dreams for Clark College and how I might fit into his plans. While he was sharing these concepts with me, he asked me to consider becoming a part of his Clark College team. I thought and prayed about it, then gladly accepted.

When it appeared that I would be employed at Clark College, the institution owned a little house around the corner from Dr. Blake's where I could set up Muriel and the children when they came down to Atlanta. By the time I got myself moved into the house, he had given me a job at Clark College. This house proved to be inadequate for a family of four; Muriel and I had to get a larger house. To our good fortune, an airline pilot was leaving town; he sold us his house on Kathryn Court, and we have been living there ever since. I don't think I'll ever get Muriel to leave that house. After we got firmly settled, President Elias Blake asked me to become the Dean of Students at Clark – a job that put me in charge of athletics, registration, financial aid, student issues, housing and other areas that a Dean is responsible for. He knew me when we worked together at ISE and so he knew that I had the skills, not only to be the Dean, but also to develop and manage the Head Start Program.

The Head Start Program was sponsored by the federal government and was created for children to get a head start on the first grade. We wrote a grant and received funding to offer this program of preparing children for beginning school. In addition to being the Dean, I was the Executive Director of Head Start and had a number of able associates who did the day to day work. Together we located six sites in Atlanta where we could house the Head Start program; several hundred children participated in it. We began the first program on the campus of Clark College, and then we occupied several schools that had been closed. In one location, we had the Head Start Program in a church. Perhaps we would have used more churches, but the federal guidelines established for the program were so stringent that most church facilities did not meet the standards. The guidelines included certain numbers of bathrooms, certain sized toilets, a proper amount of light, approved cooking facilities and handicap accessibility. With the funds that we received we were able to remodel over ten schools and enroll over 2000 kids.

I spent six wonderful years at Clark College, and then the Morehouse School of Medicine invited me to be the Director of the Health Promotion Resource Center. This research center examined diseases that disproportionately affected poor, rural Georgians in negative ways. My specific assignment was to educate communities and companies about major diseases that impacted the health of poor people. The health awareness and education program included teaching about cardiovascular diseases, hypertension, cancer, HIV AIDS, renal diseases and extreme stress. From 1984 to 1999 I was involved with Clark College and the School of Medicine at Morehouse; these were significant years for Morehouse and for me because of the work I was doing and the relationships that I was establishing. I was finally in my element, my calling, fulfilling the compelling force which governed my life to make life more endurable for the masses.

I became director of Health Promotion Resource Center in the Department of Community Health and Preventive Medicine Morehouse Medical School. I was under the tutelage of Dr. Dan Blumenthal, who was Chairman and Professor and the Director of Community Health and Preventive Medicine. We were responsible for educating people on health prevention techniques. Our task was to teach young women who were pregnant and knew very little about how to care for themselves and protect the fetus they were carrying. The information we were disseminating was urgent; our message needed to be heard. Because of the timeliness of our efforts, we coordinated faith communities, civic groups and civic organizations to assist in sharing our message. Our aim was not to rush into emergency situations, but to offer preventive care that would ward off an emergency. Postnatal care also included diet and exercise, which was also about prevention.

As I look back I realize that we were able to accomplish a great deal in student preparation at Clark College, now Clark Atlanta University, and help improve the overall health of those who live on the margins of our society.

CHAPTER SEVEN

✪

I Am Amazed at My Pastoral Ministry

IN 1984 I WAS THE DEAN OF STUDENTS at Clark College. At that time, I was attending the Ebenezer Baptist Church, where I taught Sunday school. Dr. Joseph L. Roberts appointed me as a pulpit associate at the Ebenezer Baptist Church of Atlanta, Georgia. One day, Dr. Roberts informed me of the pulpit vacancy at the Providence Missionary Baptist Church, which was located in John Hope Homes near the Atlanta University Center.

The Providence Missionary Baptist Church had a long, venerated history. From the beginning it has been closely connected with Morehouse, Spelman, Morris Brown and Clark Colleges. Dr. Benjamin Elijah Mays, president of Morehouse College, was also one of the distinguished members of the congregation. The church's congregation was considered highly educated, and they had always taken a great interest in the surrounding community. This interest was expressed in a variety of outreach ministries. Many of the activities and programs were structured to meet the needs of the people from John Hope Homes. This Atlanta Housing Authority community was not exclusively for persons lacking in culture and income; many of the residents in these homes were well educated and had decent incomes. In fact, many of the professors and administrators in the colleges around the church lived in the community and attended Providence.

In the Baptist tradition, a church seeking a pastor sends out a statement signifying that a particular church is available. The church usually conducts a survey of the congregation regarding the kind of pastor they want. They include in the statement the qualifications that they are seeking in a new pastor. The search committee, which the congregation organizes from members within the church, generally includes deacons and trustees, plus young and old representatives from the various church organizations. The search committee represents a healthy cross-section of the congregation. The committee decides on a time frame within which a candidate must respond. The committee outlines all the gifts and skills that they expect from the candidate, and he or she must answer their questions on the application before it is submitted. A congregation may send out a hundred or two hundred applications for the pastorate position.

As the resumes come in, the committee reads all of them and prayerfully considers who should be called to the church. When they have narrowed the number down to five or six candidates, they interview them face to face and listen to them share the word of God with the congregation. The candidate may preach and/or teach a Bible study. The committee and representatives then talk with the candidate about his/her gifts for the type of ministry they feel would be most appropriate for the church. After the preaching, teaching and interviews, the committee generally narrows the list to a few prospects who are invited to return and preach a second sermon.

A hundred ministers may make application for a particular church. There were already over one hundred applicants when I submitted my resume. In this instance, the search committee cut the list down to two people. Those two candidates were Reverend Dr. Aaron Parker and me, Gerald L. Durley. For over a hundred years the Providence Church had never had a pastor who did not graduate from Morehouse College. Aaron Parker was a Morehouse graduate, and at the time he was teaching religion at Morehouse College. He had the reputation of being a very prominent preacher, scholar and teacher. Both he and I had preached at Providence and on the night that the vote was to be taken, there were one hundred people present to vote for their choice. The counters of the first ballot came back with a report that out of the one hundred persons who had voted, fifty votes were cast for Parker and fifty votes for Durley. Rather than delay the vote until another meeting, the search committee suggested a second vote right then and there. They discussed each candidate openly, then passed out small slips of paper on which all the members wrote the candidate of their choice. The final vote was fifty-three to forty-seven in favor of Durley. With no reflection on either candidate, God will always have the final say when the congregation is praying and trusting in Him.

A few days later, I was notified that I had been called to be the pastor of Providence Missionary Baptist Church. In so doing I was breaking my promise to Muriel, that I would never be a preacher in a local congregation. I really did not see myself as a preacher in a church; rather, I saw myself as a person who wanted to make a difference in the John Hope Homes community where Providence was located. For me, the Providence Church was the ideal place to have the kind of ministry that God placed in my vision. I believed that if we preached the gospel of Jesus Christ and lived it on a daily basis, that it would be a strong witness to the whole community. If we followed the implications of this message, it would create a community of strong people who would take their place in the larger community both economically, politically and educationally. Citizens like these could make a "blessed community" that was culturally and spiritually mature. God sent me to the right place. He knew where He wanted me to serve. I felt that it was a place where we could preach the gospel, live the gospel and transform the community. I didn't know how all of this would come together, but I never forgot what Dean Jones told me the day that the men from AAA got my car out of the snow and ice – "God does His work through people." I knew then and I know now that when God calls, we can accept or reject His calling. I accepted the call to Providence whole-heartedly.

What a Church Needs

When I became pastor of Providence church, I believed that for it to be really meaningful, we had to focus on seriously understanding the Bible. At that time, the congregation was older and needed young adults with growing families. It seemed to me that the congregation needed and wanted an infusion of enthusiasm through new members. We also had a desire to nurture the spiritual growth of the older members. In addition to developing relevant Bible study, we examined our worship music. And we decided to explore different forms of music. Music for us was ministry, not mere entertainment. Music became another way to infuse and excite God's word into the heart of the congregation. We formed several new choirs: a youth choir, a gospel choir, and a sanctuary choir, all of which had the goal of creating a warm, spiritual environment for the worship of God. There is no substitute for good old, honest enthusiasm. Bible study and vital worship experiences began to release a new energy in the worshipers.

Our Community Outreach

As new life began to break forth in the church, the members expressed this overflow of the Spirit through mission work in our community. One of our first programs centered on the distribution of food to those in our neighborhood and beyond who were in need. Every week, we supplied food to more than a hundred families to help supplement their food supply; without the food that we passed out, those families would have gone hungry. In recent years, I began to notice a difference in those who came to receive food. The difference was in the mixture of the crowd; in the early days, many were poor people who required assistance. Twenty-five years later, the large group of people who came on Fridays seeking food assistance was from various socioeconomic sections of society. There is certainly a contrast with those who came for help in the beginning. Most of the people who continue to come to the food program today get enough food for the week.

Once a month, we fill one hundred and sixty boxes with food for seniors, which lasts them for one month. We are able to operate this large food distribution program because of food programs established by the Atlanta Food Bank. Our church received referrals from the Department of Family and Children Services, the Red Cross and other churches. We have assisted people with food who have been stranded in our city and have no money to purchase food. We attempt to provide them enough food to meet their needs for a week. Our goal is to distribute as much food as we can, until we exhaust the supply. To respond to a broad range of needs, our boxes often contain Pampers, cleaning supplies, paper products and other non-food items. The church shares about a ton of food each week. Those responsible for this ministry keep very strict records because each month we are required to give the Atlanta Food Bank and other suppliers an accounting of all the food that we distribute. At the end of each month we report to the Food Bank the amount of food we distributed and the number of persons served.

In addition to food, we realized that there were also those in need of clothing. We invited the church's members to bring new or slightly used clothes to donate. These clothes are placed in a section of the church that we call our Clothes Closet. After completing their food requests, many visit the Clothes Closet to select appropriate clothing. Sometimes a man will turn in ten or fifteen shirts that have gotten too small or an equal number of pants that no longer fit. The shirts and pants are still fairly new and can be of value to someone who may have fallen on tough times.

With respect to children, many perfectly good clothes were donated to bless hundreds of school children. These were practically new clothes that a son or daughter had outgrown. Grandparents buy clothes for grandchildren that never get delivered, so they often bring them to our Clothes Closet brand new. The Clothes Closet also collects and purchases sweaters and coats for winter months. There is no price on the clothing; people just take what they need. We only ask that they not take the clothes and sell them, but that they wear them or give them to someone else who can use them.

In another effort to make a difference, we joined hands with the Atlanta Housing Authority to upgrade the housing facilities in the neighborhood. For example, we purchased a house across the street from the church and repaired it so that it could house women who had been abused; we envisioned it to be a transition house. This house provided space enough to handle three women and their children at one time. In this program we partnered with Spelman College and Clark Atlanta University to encourage volunteer students to take care of the children from 3:00 p.m. to 6:00 p.m. when the mothers returned from work. Without this assistance the women could not have been employed. The person responsible for this ministry collaborated with the Labor Department to provide employment for the women. We made it clear from the beginning that the transition house would not become a permanent home. The goal was to move toward self-sufficiency. Generally, it took families from six to nine months to make the transition back to some level of assuming personal responsibility for their own well being.

As we opened our hearts to serve others, we discovered numerous opportunities to be a source of assistance to many. Our team thought that it was important to provide families with toys and gifts for Christmas. We discovered two viable ways to conduct this ministry. We originally served families in John Hope Homes and collected toys from the U.S. Marine Corps. The Atlanta Falcons sponsored a "Toys for Tots" day in mid-December, and Falcon fans provided thousands of small toys for children. A second resource for collecting toys and clothes was the Angel Tree Program. The members bring toys to be given to families, and businesses would also donate toys and gifts. We decided that all the toys and gifts we give to families for Christmas must be new. In the Angel Tree program, we gave various members of the congregation the names of children and their sizes for clothing, which was purchased specifically for that child.

Along with these ministries that provided tangibles like food, clothing and shelter, we found it necessary to provide non-material needs. For example, when crime and domestic violence occurred, we provided counseling to assist the abused as well as assisting those who were guilty of these offenses. Providence Church became a source of feeding, clothing, counseling and deepening the spiritual awareness of people in our neighborhood. The congregation became a trusted, integral part of the community, which I believe is the role and purpose of the Church.

On Fair Street we assisted in establishing a police sub-station to bring law enforcement closer to the residents. Having a sub-station in our community gave our members and persons outside the church an opportunity to develop a different, more enriched relationship with the police who patrolled the area. As a congregation that cared about the appearance of our community, we spent a full month cleaning up an area for a playground and locating places for various kinds of sports – baseball, basketball and soccer. We approached the Housing Authority, and they allowed us to use an entire building to house our counseling services, referral agency, employment assistance, and other services needed by the residents. The tenant association worked closely with us, enabling us to recognize and respond to their needs. As one might expect, when we kept reaching out to people around us and responding to their needs, our congregation began to grow. Growth in membership was important to us because we knew that lives were being changed, pain was being alleviated, and many of the people began to see and understand the power of what Jesus Christ meant when he said, "Love thy neighbor." Jesus' Sermon on the Mount was being seen and realized every day.

Having ministered in this community for a number of years, we decided to partner with Johnson Ferry Baptist Church, a very large and prominent white Southern Baptist church. They worshiped with us in our building, and we began to worship with them in theirs. They joined with us in multiple ministries, which was a blessing to the community. Joining forces with Clark College, we offered adult literacy courses. If the people we were assisting were to become personally responsible and seek employment, we knew that they needed basic education. Our church didn't offer many youth educational programs because we didn't want to compete with the teaching done by the Atlanta City Public Schools; it was more important for us to provide after-school tutoring and mentorship programs.

Acquiring a significant response from groups around the church results from the viability of a congregation and its service to the community. When the residents in the community felt comfortable asking to use our church building for community meetings, we knew we had come to a new place of acceptance. Our church made the decision that the building would always be open for meetings like Alcoholics Anonymous, as well as member and non-member weddings and funerals.

We decided to be available to our friends and neighbors. Building a relationship of trust through open communication was probably the most important effort of our first three or four years at Providence. We wanted to be perceived as servants of God willing to do His will with and for everyone. Every Saturday hundreds of people lined up for our bag lunch program, which met the needs of children who did not have lunch on Saturday or Sunday. We were pleased that we could supplement their food for the weekend. They would have been hungry apart from this program.

The president of the tenant association, Mrs. Vernon Mobley, was an integral part of guiding the church to a positive response to the needs around us. Leaders in the church were a welcomed part of the tenant association board, and she encouraged us to be a part of the community. For a long time there had been a significant relationship between the tenants at John Hope Homes and the congregation at Providence. Originally, it was necessary to establish trust because a congregation in a housing project has the potential to create strained relationships. Miscommunication can breed distrust and possibly destructive consequences; good, open communication leads to the opposite – peaceful relations that enable productivity and provide confidence and hope among all participants. In fact, we became a family that depended on each other and shared mutual concerns.

Other Forms of Ministry
In the early years of my ministry at Providence, HIV-AIDS was being diagnosed with greater frequency. Once at the end of a worship service, a mother literally ran into the sanctuary and came forward asking me to come pray for her daughter. Still garbed in my black clergy robe, I ran behind her to her apartment and followed her upstairs. I saw her daughter in the bed hiding under the covers. She was about nineteen years old and was lying in a fetal position; she only weighed fifty-nine pounds. She was diagnosed with AIDS and had learned that there was no treatment. We were confused, hurt, and prayerful. I didn't know what to do or what to pray for, but I did know who to pray to.

Honestly, I was frightened, so I asked the mother, "What can I do?"

She said, "Pray for my daughter; she needs to be healed." By this time people were lined up outside the house waiting to see what the young preacher would do for the dying daughter. Frankly, I was overwhelmed by the confidence they had in me and my ability to pray. They really believed that I could do something to heal this young lady who was so far gone. The faith they had in me taught me to have more faith in God to do what He said He would do if we asked and believed.

I asked the mother, "Do you believe God can heal?"

Between her yelling and screaming, she said, "Yes, I believe!"

I began to pray, but I must confess, I was full of doubt when I prayed. But most everyone both in and outside the apartment believed that the young lady was going to get well. I was amazed that the people who did not even attend the church thanked me and patted me on the back in gratitude. Both they and the mother were pleased with what I had done. The fact that I took the time to go to this distraught woman's apartment meant that I, and the church, appreciated them as human beings. I regret to say that the young lady died that evening.

I had mixed emotions. I wondered whether God heard my prayer or if I had expected too much. The people trusted me so deeply and they felt that I trusted in God so much that God would work a miracle through me. I now realize that there are times that everything is in God's hands and not in mine. That experience, however, resulted in the funeral service being conducted at Providence. Losing that young woman in such a dramatic fashion opened up new pathways for dialogue around preventive health care in our community. Hands-on involvement engenders trust and greatly enhances communication. God's ways are not our ways.

Some moments in the life of a congregation are comical and sad at the same time. On New Year's Eve we conducted a Watch Night service. It was our tradition to "pray in" the New Year. Usually, we began about 11:00 p.m. and ended about 12:30 a.m. We generally drank some hot chocolate and then drove home. During my third Watch Night service, we heard a noise like firecrackers popping. We mused and figured that others also were bringing in the New Year in their own way. Later, we learned that they were not shooting off fireworks; they were actually firing guns! After that, to protect our members we decided to stay in the building until 1:00 or 1:15 a.m. The extra waiting proved positive for our congregation because it allowed us to pray for an extra forty-five minutes.

At Providence we had a very small building that had one men's restroom and one women's restroom. The men's restroom was right across from my office at the bottom of several steps. I had a very small office. When I finished preaching and greeting the congregation after the service, I would walk down the steps and into my office. While we were upstairs worshiping, we allowed people from the community to use the bathroom across from my office. Occasionally, people who had had a little too much to drink came in and used the washroom, and on a few occasions they stopped up the toilet.

One Sunday, after preaching the sermon, I bounced down the steps toward my office to change clothes, when I stumbled and slipped on water that had pooled at the bottom of the steps. As I sat there in my robe, I realized that the water was from a toilet that had over-flowed. I heard myself saying, "God, why am I here? What am I doing in this place?" But I got up, and continued on. I had those question answered for me, though, years later. One of the members said to me, "You are here, Reverend Durley, because God sent you to us and we love you and you love us."

There was a gentleman who lived in our community whom I had known for some time. He had been in rehab but didn't overcome his addictions. On one particular night, he had gotten drunk and was locked up in jail. It required a hundred dollars to get him out. I raised the money and paid his fine. We got into my car, and I planned to take him home. I felt pretty good because I had been God's angel to him. But in that moment, he looked me in the face and asked, "Why did you wake me up and drag me out here? I was doing okay in my cell. Don't you realize there's only one God and you are not Him? So why didn't you let me finish my good night's sleep and get out in the morning?" One learns over time that you can't help people until they are ready to help themselves.

From this effort to do a good deed for a man, I learned a lesson that has helped me through many similar situations. When I have tried to help people and they don't appreciate it, I recall the lesson that I learned from that experience. I say to myself, "I am not God, and I can only do what I can do." This man eventually became one of my closest friends and confidants during my ministry.

Pastors: Surrogate Parents

America has some great preachers, but we are in need of great pastors. Pastors must be prepared to serve as surrogate fathers and surrogate mothers. They become the resource for encouraging new levels of self-esteem, self-worth, social values, principles and fortitude for members to survive the delivery of difficult news. At times, all pastors need to do for a young generation is to recognize them and simply speak a word of encouragement. These are the attitudes and skills that should be experienced daily in a family environment, but this becomes difficult in a single-parent family with so many other overwhelming responsibilities.

In view of this crying need, as the pastor at Providence I became all things to all people in a variety of circumstances. At times I felt so unworthy and ill-equipped to fulfill this role, but I am now thoroughly convinced that whenever you reach out with genuine faith and integrity, God will provide you with what is needed. God not only gives you the words, but He will also give you the energy to do what is required in any situation. The Bible says, "God does not give us the spirit of fear, but of power and of love and of a sound mind." (II Timothy 1:7) Those who work in underserved communities must lay aside any and all fear of unforeseen circumstances. If we serve with pure love, the decisions we make will not be interpreted as malicious. Love conquers ignorance when one is truly sincere.

For example, it is important to help children with social graces that are generally learned from the family and the broader society. Social graces may be overlooked in less affluent homes because time is spent on making a living. I remember a time when I was asked to deliver a speech to an elementary school's graduating class. The aim of my address was to teach the young men the importance of appropriate dress for the appropriate occasion. When I was scheduled to give this speech, the principal requested that all the young boys wear a necktie to the graduation exercise. When I came into the room where the fellows were waiting to march in, forty-five young men were standing before me. I noticed that every young man had a tie in his hand, but none of them had their ties on. Too many of us do not understand the absence of training that our youth lack at home – like being taught when and where to wear a tie. As I examined these boys, many of them had adult ties because they did not own a child's tie. I asked one of the boys, "Why don't you put on your tie?" The little boy said, "Mister, I don't know how to tie a tie." The kid next to him said he didn't know how to tie a tie either. A resounding shout came from the whole group, "We don't know how to tie our ties."

As I reflected on their responses, I wondered how many of these young men had an adult man in his life. I said to the class, "Today, before we go into your graduation exercise, we are going to learn how to tie a tie." I enlisted the help of a couple of coaches in the room, and we enjoyed teaching the young men how to tie their ties. I went through the exercise of tying a necktie, a demonstration for each to follow. When every young man had on his tie, they all had broad grins and a joyous sense of accomplishment. That experience was one of the highlights of my entire life. There is astounding joy in sharing and giving. Not to mention, we had fun!

When we walked out of the room and into the auditorium, I heard the parents cheering as each young man marched out with his tie on. They walked with a sense of regal pride, and the young girls cheered them on as they looked around with warm smiles. When I got up to give the speech, I said to the group of young men, "You look good!" I asked everyone in the bleachers – parents, grandparents and the young girls – to do something very important. I said, "I want all of you to stand and give these good-looking young men a round of applause." I began to clap, the audience began to clap, and the boys stood up and gave each other high fives. I cried as the audience clapped louder and louder. It doesn't take much time to instill pride, just a willingness to care.

Many homes, no matter what the economic condition, don't have a complete set of silverware and serving dishes. Many young children do not even know the names of the serving dishes or the appropriate utensils for eating certain foods. Many people are accustomed to using a knife and a fork, and that is the extent of their knowledge. I wanted our children to be knowledgeable about dining etiquette. To respond to this issue, every year I took a group of children to a downtown hotel and requested the hotel to set a table with the full range of silverware and accompanying serving pieces. Before we began eating the prepared meal, I stood up and explained to the children which utensils to use for each dish. Then I explained the purpose for the salad fork, butter knife, dessert spoon, teaspoon and tablespoon. I demonstrated to them how to cut meat, how to slowly eat their vegetables and when to use their napkins. I explained to them when and how they were to use what was before them. Many of them knew what to do, but lack of exposure to the broader culture can socially cripple our youth.

It was always a highlight of the evening to see each one of them using the right spoon at the appropriate time and with the correct dish. The focal point of this excursion was to provide a learning exercise that would make them comfortable when they found themselves in a formal dinner setting. With this experience they learned how to conduct themselves and what was expected of them in this environment. I have found that the difference in success and failure stems from having been exposed to proper etiquette in social gatherings, not how intelligent or smart you may be – but your exposure!

While we were waiting to eat at one of our visits to a hotel, I heard a roar of laughter from the children. I went out to see what was going on, and the excited children were running up and down on what they called "moving steps". They were playing a game, competing with each other to see who could get off "the moving steps" without falling. Of course, they were playing on the escalator. I laughed to myself at how we often take simple things for granted. Where would they have ever seen an escalator? There were no escalators in the small neighborhood stores where their parents shopped. We talked about escalators, how they transport people from one level to another and why large busy buildings needed escalators. In life, success depends not only on how smart you are but what you have been exposed to and who did the exposing. If people put you down or make you feel inferior, your learning experience will be negative. Learning is at its best when people share new information with you and don't make you feel inferior. You cannot teach another without learning something yourself. The educational process is a mutual adventure.

In our church we instituted a program to teach children basic courtesy. Words like "I'm sorry," "Excuse me," "Forgive me," "Thank you." These basic words make a difference in how people respond to you and how you relate to other people. One day, when I was instructing a group of boys and girls on tactful words to use, a little girl about five or six years old got up to leave the room. When she accidentally stepped on my foot, she looked at me with a certain sense of pride and said, "Thank you." The little boy sitting next to me blurted out to the girl, "You are supposed to say 'excuse me' when you step on someone's foot." I took him aside and said to the young man, "You are exactly right," and he beamed with appreciation. I then told the young lady, "Thank you for thanking me; at least you were thinking about me, and that makes me feel good." Every congregation should make plans to teach people how to be successful in the world today, as well as a life with God in the great hereafter!

Building a Home for Senior Citizens

When we speak about the Gerald L. Durley Providence Manor, it is necessary to describe the vision and the inspiration for the beginning of this great dream. A residence for senior citizens was an idea which gave us a way to serve the seniors in our community. Providence had always been concerned and actively involved in caring for the homeless, the hungry, those without clothes, working with youth, fatherhood programs, drug programs, pregnancy programs and anti-violence programs. With all these creative ministries under way, we believed it was necessary for us to develop a response to the seniors in our neighborhood. We resolved that seniors are the foundation upon which our very lives are being lived. We owe our seniors a major debt of gratitude.

I had been reading about a Housing and Urban Development program called 202 funds. This federal money was set aside to assist 501(c) (3) organizations in building housing for seniors. I brought this idea to the Board of Trustees; they said that this would be a great ministry for Providence Church. In our community we found a parcel of land that we could buy for $387,000. We purchased the land and began to develop a proposal to submit to the Housing and Urban Development program (HUD). The first year we were not funded; the second year we worked with a consulting firm that helped us refine our proposal. We had a very high rating, but we still were not funded. We were somewhat dispirited, but we believed that if we were doing unselfish work to the glory of God by trying to assist his people here on earth, that this project would eventually be funded. We refined the proposal and submitted it a third time.

We were notified that we should make some positive reference to the current administration in Washington with respect to their working with African-American communities. I felt, at the time, that the current administration was doing very little to help African-American seniors in urban areas with housing. Therefore, I could not write a cover letter saying that the administration was actively helping African-American communities when I didn't believe it to be true, especially when our proposal for senior housing had been turned down three times. One has to be true to one's personal convictions.

When we were not funded for a fourth time, the trustees began to question if this was a viable project. Every year we were paying a great deal of money in taxes on the land. Being turned down a fourth time forced us to face a vote on whether to sell the property or persist in seeking funding. I received an appointment and had a frank discussion with the regional HUD office. At the conclusion of our meeting, I will admit, I was extremely frustrated. I decided to handle my frustrations by praying for the regional representatives. At the conclusion of the prayer, I thanked them for the meeting. I left with the assumption that we would not be funded for the fifth time. I know that a person should believe that his prayer will be answered, but I had very little faith that we would get funded. That Saturday when the trustees met, the issue of selling the land did not come up. On Monday morning I left the country traveling with the World Pilgrims to Turkey and Israel. While I was in Israel, the trustees from the church sent a message that we had been funded. I received the news with total faithful disbelief – an oxymoron. When I got home from the trip, we began putting all the required details together so that we could begin construction on the senior citizens home. God knows when the timing is right. We are taught patience and dependence on God through disappointments.

We had to create a new board for the Providence Learning Center and Development Corporation. The chair of that board was also the chair of the Board of Trustees of the church. The moving force for this project was attorney Michael Tyler. We could not have completed this effort without him. This new board had the responsibility of hiring architects, construction workers and a contractor to manage the project.

The building began with the groundbreaking attended by such well-known civic leaders as Roy Barnes, Governor of the State of Georgia; the Mayor of Atlanta, Kasim Reed; the President of the City Council, Ceasar Mitchell; Councilmen Jim Maddox and Ivory Young and several State Representatives. The building was completed in an unbelievable amount of time, only eighteen months. Our new senior citizens residence contained forty-six one-bedroom units, ten of which were handicapped accessible. Each resident had a living room, bedroom and kitchen, and all the units were outfitted with appliances as well.

The second floor had a recreation room. We also worked out a plan for every resident to have a membership to the Walter and Andrew Young YMCA down the street. Behind the building we developed a walking track, and we set aside space for individual gardening. There was ample room on each floor for a sitting area so that residents had privacy to sit and converse with family and friends in private.

While we were under construction, we announced the date of the opening. To live in the senior citizens facility, a person had to be at least sixty-two years of age and not make over $25,000 a year. To be in compliance with the law, each resident had to meet all of the guidelines to become a resident. We hired a resident manager who worked from nine to five and had another manager to live in overnight. She worked from five in the evening to nine in the morning. We also hired a maintenance person. When we opened the facility, we had 90 percent occupancy. A few weeks later we had 100 percent of the building filled. After two years of occupancy we had a long waiting list. The Gerald L. Durley Providence Manor is considered a model for senior residency in the southeast. When the building was opened, not one of the residents was a member of Providence. Since moving in, six of them have become members of the church, but it was not a prerequisite for acquiring residency. A majority of the residents are women; about 30 percent of the residents are men.

When I review all the things we were able to do at Providence Missionary Baptist Church, I am very grateful. After spending time reviewing and organizing the congregation, we were able to make a lasting impact on our community. I'm grateful for the privilege I had to serve as pastor of so many wonderful people. My ministry, however, was not limited to the congregation, but extended into the social and political life of Atlanta.

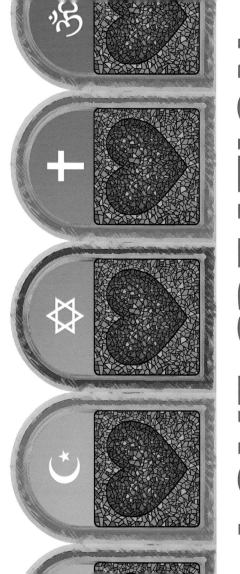

LOVE CREATION

Dear Senator,

As a person of faith, I believe we have a moral obligation to future generations to leave them a planet that is not polluted or damaged by climate change. I support America's transition away from dirty energy sources to clean energy and a brighter future. Power plants are the largest source of carbon pollution in the U.S.

We must act now if we are to have any hope of preserving the Earth's bounty for future generations. **Please support the EPA's Carbon Pollution Standards for New and Existing Power Plants.** Thank you in advance for doing your part.

Sincerely,

Print Name _____

City, State ZIP _____

Congregation (optional) _____

34 cents

Hon. _____

United States Senate

Washington, DC 20510

Interfaith Power & Light
A Religious Response to Global Warming
www.interfaithpowerandlight.org

Family

Muriel, Hasan, Nia and Gerald

Gerald and LeRoy Durley (dad)

The family with Rev. Dr. and Mrs. Joseph Lowery and Rev. Dr. C.T. Vivian

The Peace Corps

The Peace Corps: Service in Nigeria

Speaking at Home and Abroad

At Providence

In Turkey

In Georgia

Speaking at Home and Abroad

Campaigning for Senator Obama (With Rev. C.T. Vivian and Rev. Joseph E. Lowery)

Leading a March for Health and Peace

Co-Chair Of the Atlanta Billy Graham Crusade

With Rev. Billy Graham

With Revs. Alexander, Graham and Harrington

Trinity Broadcasting Network
in Amsterdam

National + International Leadership

With Mayor Shirley Franklin, Rev. Joseph Lowery, Ambassador Andrew Young, Congressman John Lewis, Gov. Roy Barnes

With Jane Fonda and environmentalists

With Imam El-Amin and Rabbi Segal

National + International Leadership

With Ambassador Andrew Young and Mrs. Coretta Scott King

With World Pilgrims in Turkey (Muslims, Christians & Jews)

National + International Leadership

With dinner hosts in Istanbul, Turkey

With Mother Teresa Sisters in Turkey

With Interfaith group in Turkey

National + International Leadership

With Congressman John Lewis and Concerned Black Clergy in D.C.

With Mayor Maynard Jackson, Ambassador Andrew Young, Rep. Bob Holmes,
Mr. Jessie Hill and Mr. Herman Russell

Presidents + Politicians

With Gov. Roy Barnes

With President Bill Clinton

With President and Mrs. Jimmy Carter

Presidents + Politicians

With President Obama

With Hillary Clinton and Michelle Nunn

With Mayors Jackson and Franklin

My Dearest Friend and Ardent Supporter

With my wife, Muriel

At the unveiling of the portrait at
Morehouse College

CHAPTER EIGHT

✪

I Am Amazed at My Ministry in Greater Atlanta

As the pastor of Providence Missionary Baptist Church, I was fully engaged in church work, and at the same time also heavily involved in work for the city and state. It is my belief that there is little difference between serving in the church and working among the various institutions in society which serve the welfare of humanity. As far as I was concerned, we must all work as one. In 1994, I was invited to be one of the chairs for the Billy Graham Crusade, a task that involved both the church and the community. The Crusade offered a fantastic opportunity to create an interface between the church and the community. I had already established those connections to a degree; however, the Crusade gave me more visibility and increased my strategies to systematically integrate the religious, social, and political agendas of Atlanta.

The Billy Graham Crusade in Atlanta

When I was first asked to be a part of the Billy Graham Crusade in Atlanta, I was deeply concerned and rather hesitant. My hesitation arose from the fact that Dr. Graham, in my mind, was an extreme fundamentalist, a person who spoke to segregated groups in South Africa and served as a personal chaplain to U.S. presidents who I felt did not always have the best interests of African-Americans and African-American communities at heart. For the most part, I felt that the presidents he served were politically conservative.

When Dan Southern, a member of the Billy Graham team, came

to Atlanta, he explained to me that they wanted a diverse, integrated group of people at the Crusade every night. The local group in charge of planning the Crusade suggested that leaders from the Graham team speak with me about involving the African-American community in order to enlist the support of the broader, more diverse community in the Crusade. My immediate reaction was, "I've got too much on my plate already." They continued to talk with me about the expansiveness of what Dr. Graham desired to accomplish, not in the U.S. alone, but also around the world; he was not only speaking about salvation, but he was aware and concerned about social issues as well. To allay my concerns, members of the Graham team urged me to fly with them to Cleveland, Ohio to observe a Billy Graham Crusade, meet Dr. Graham, and personally ask him any questions I had about his evangelistic intentions in Atlanta. I reluctantly accepted their offer and challenge.

When we landed in Cleveland, Ohio, we went directly to the big arena. I was taken behind the stadium where Dr. Graham's trailer was parked. We entered the trailer, and I met Dr. Billy Graham for the first time. When we entered his trailer, he was sitting behind his desk preparing the evening sermon. As we walked in, I was awestruck. My sense of awe did not come upon me because of Dr. Graham's reputation, but because of his demeanor. He was humble, he was receptive, and he knew my name! We sat down and he welcomed me to the Crusade in Cleveland. With a quiet smile he said that he looked forward to coming to Atlanta. He appreciated my willingness to work with his staff in Atlanta and promised his complete cooperation with achieving our mutual goal – inclusion. That night in Cleveland, I closely observed him. I heard his message about racial inclusiveness. He spoke about breaking down barriers of all types: class barriers, gender barriers, as well as racial barriers. His message was constructed on a liberation theology motif. I was impressed with all that happened to me that night, and that experience converted me to become an avid supporter of Dr. Graham and the Crusade in Atlanta.

As a member of the Crusade's leadership team, I would be working with the ministerial planning team. Two other men composed the three-man ministerial committee: Dr. Frank Harrington and Dr.

Cameron Alexander. The three of us began meeting regularly with the Graham staff; they assigned me to work with those in the Black community. I was also asked to chair the Love in Action Committee. Every Graham Crusade had a Love in Action Committee which was allotted 10 percent of the funds raised during the Crusade. These funds were later invested in the city to continue the evangelism outreach after the Crusade. In Atlanta the 10 percent contribution amounted to about $200,000 dollars. With those funds the Crusade purchased two mobile medical units used for medical outreach to all persons throughout the city. Those two units, which supplied medical services from hospitals to various areas in and around Atlanta, are still in service today. Thanks be to God for Dr. Graham and the contribution he continues to make to our city through that very generous gift.

The Crusade was a striking success; every night 70,000 people crowded into the Georgia Dome to hear the gospel proclaimed in word and song. The leaders of the Crusade were amazed and very pleased at how many people from the African-American community came to hear Dr. Graham and how they expressed their appreciation for his messages. One of the payoffs for me, while serving in the Crusade, was meeting and working with a significant number of African-Americans across Atlanta. In addition to meeting a number of African-Americans at the Crusade, I also became acquainted with a genuine core group of white Christians from Beecher Hills Baptist Church. God is so awesome.

At the time we, members of the Providence Baptist Church, were negotiating with the trustees of the Beecher Hills Baptist Church about the purchase of their property. Many of the Beecher Hills Baptist Church members wanted to attend the Billy Graham Crusade. Since we were interested in purchasing their facility and I was responsible for building attendance at the Crusade, I figured Providence and Beecher Hills could work toward mutual goals. One night, while at Beecher Hills, we were talking about Providence purchasing their property and they asked me if I could get them tickets to attend the Billy Graham Crusade. I looked at them with a questioning eye and said, "Well, I will attempt to get you some tickets. How many do you need?"

They said, "Do you think you could get as many as fifteen or twenty tickets?"

Sheepishly, I said, "It might be difficult, but I will try."

The source of my confidence came from my knowledge that we sought to distribute 70,000 tickets each night. They were grateful that I would attempt to acquire twenty tickets, but when I gave them fifty tickets and provided a bus to take them to the Crusade, they were more than appreciative. We not only drove them to the arena, we went down under the grandstands and led them up a series of steps right in front of the stage. They had front row seats to see and listen to Billy Graham, George Beverly Shea and Cliff Barrows. They were so excited that they said, "Dr. Durley, let's talk about making definitive arrangements about Providence purchasing our facility." After that, we sat down and talked about price and a payment schedule. With a gentle suggestion from me, Dr. Graham sent the Beecher Hills trustees a letter thanking them for working with our congregation. Dr. Graham subtly enhanced our evangelistic outreach and thereby helped to change Atlanta.

During the Crusade, Dan Southern and I took Dr. Graham to visit one of the most prominent ministers in the city. Most people came to meet Dr. Graham at his hotel or at a designated luncheon venue, but to speak to this particular minister, he said, "No, I want to go to this pastor's office and meet with him there." When we entered this prominent minister's office, the receptionist said, "He will be with you in a few minutes." Dr. Graham, Dan and I sat patiently for thirty minutes. While we were waiting, we talked about the Crusade, about the minister we were waiting to speak with and our anticipated involvement of African-Americans who would be in attendance. Dr. Graham spoke very kindly and patiently for another fifteen minutes. Finally, I suggested that maybe we should leave and come back another time. Dr. Graham said, "No, I think we should just wait." About that time the door opened and the minister warmly greeted us. He apologized profusely for the long delay, explaining that one of the members of his congregation had had a fatal accident. He stated compassionately, "I have to take care of my members, Dr. Graham; I'm sorry to have kept you waiting." He then invited us to come into his office and sit down for a conversation. I was enlightened and inspired watching those two spiritual giants exchange views about the Kingdom of God. When they finished talking, we got in the car and Dr. Graham said, "What a wonderful day we are having." I truly love and respect that brother.

Dr. Frank Harrington

I had another very interesting experience during the Crusade. One day Dr. Cameron Alexander and I visited with Dr. Frank Harrington at Peachtree Presbyterian Church of Atlanta, where he was the senior pastor. We had planned to discuss ways to bring diverse sides of the community together for the Crusade. The two of us were standing in the sanctuary of the Peachtree Church when Dr. Harrington entered; he began telling us about their new organ. We stood in awe as we viewed those ornate pipes; they were beautiful. All who knew him will acknowledge that Dr. Harrington had a very keen sense of humor. He was so genuine and transparent.

He explained to us that this magnificent organ had been designed and built by a company in Germany. The Peachtree Church had bought the organ and had it shipped to Atlanta. It was assembled and installed right there in the sanctuary. Dr. Alexander and I naturally asked, "How much did an organ like that cost?" Dr. Harrington said, "It cost us about $400,000." Then he coyly relayed that the high cost had somewhat saddened him.

With tongue in cheek, Dr. Alexander and I responded, "Yes, you should have gotten a better deal than that!" Dr. Harrington said, "No, I wasn't saddened by the deal. I was sorry that it took us almost four months to pay for it." Both of us almost died laughing when we realized that it would have taken us four years or maybe forty years to purchase an organ like that. Dr. Harrington's sense of devotion, commitment, and humor solidified our intentions to make this a great Crusade.

Turning Faith Loose in the World

When the Crusade was over, Dan Southern and the other members of the Crusade team left town. While Dan was in Atlanta, he had joined a church and later became an ordained minister. I was invited to participate in his ordination service. Following his ordination, he moved to Texas and became president of the American Tract Society. Founded in 1831, it was the oldest tract society in America. This organization distributes Christian tracts all over the world. He continued, however, to serve as a consultant to the Billy Graham Crusades.

In 2000, six years after the Crusade in Atlanta, the Billy Graham Evangelistic Association planned a worldwide meeting of evangelists in Amsterdam, the Netherlands. The ministers who attended represented 185 countries; the conference drew about 10,000 participants. Franklin Graham, Billy Graham's son, was an active organizer for this conference. He explained that the gathering needed someone with an urban perspective to give insight into what the Graham Crusade could achieve in a city when there was committed collaboration. So they called me and asked if I would go to Amsterdam and share with them what we had done in Atlanta. They asked me to emphasize how we systematically merged diverse cultures during the Crusade. At that conference I met both Franklin Graham and his sister. I also had the privilege of meeting Bill Bright, who began Campus Crusade for Christ. Like the Graham Crusade, Campus Crusade for Christ was known all over the world. One evening, I had a long discussion with Bill Bright and a diverse group of ministers from around the world.

Even though I was not an evangelist, I came with a desire to learn more about how to expand my ministry around the world. I had worked in Nigeria; I had lived in Switzerland; and now, as I sat with these persons from all over the world, I began to visualize how I could participate in this global ministry. I returned to Atlanta, and for many months I remained in contact with numerous evangelists that I had met at the conference. Though I did not go and preach and teach with them, I continued to be enamored with the possibility of evangelizing in other parts of the world. God knows where He wants to use you and will prepare you for His mission for your life.

This global ministry appealed to me because in some ways it reminded me of my call to the Peace Corps thirty-six years earlier. Much of the follow-up work of the Billy Graham International Crusade involved a practical ministry – building homes, promoting healthcare issues, purifying water and working at mosquito abatement. This practical work also included nourishing diets for children and providing health supplies to villages. So it wasn't only a ministry about saving souls, but one of meeting the comprehensive needs of people, whatever they happened to be. That clear vision has not changed to this day. It has led to my involvement with World Pilgrims and engaging other secular, humanitarian-type organizations. To further demonstrate his graciousness, later on Dr. Graham showed a very personal interest in me and my family. On the day that my daughter was married, I was out in the garage with friends. Some of the other guests came out and said, "Gerald, Dr. Billy Graham is on the phone; he wants to speak with you."

Thinking they were pulling my leg, I said, "Tell him I'm busy. No, just tell him that I'm tied up." I thought they were kidding.
With their insistence, I went into the house and picked up the phone. I listened and heard the voice of Dr. Graham. He said, "May I speak with your daughter? I want to congratulate her on her wedding." Not only did he make my daughter's day a tremendous delight, but when I went back to the garage, I was admiringly accused of being "Somebody."

Faith-based Organizations

Under the umbrella of FAMA (Faith Alliance of Metro Atlanta) and World Pilgrims, I began to serve in many different ministries – speaking in synagogues, temples, churches and mosques. I continued to work with a number of 501(c) (3) organizations. The leadership of these charitable organizations invited me to actively participate in their work and speak to their constituencies. It is nearly impossible to address these groups without engaging in politics. How can we address the needs of the poor, the sick and the disenfranchised without challenging political realities? This led me to speak out forcefully in political rallies and campaigns which involved mayors, congresspersons, county and state legislators and the U.S presidential race. My life has been driven by a vision to create an environment that makes it possible for all people to reach their maximum potential. Therefore, when I speak to these various groups, I see each of them as a piece of a solvable puzzle. They must challenge unemployment, hunger, poverty, health care and education because it takes finding all of these viable solutions to modern-day issues to create the kind of environment that will provide equal opportunities for the masses.

Concerned Black Clergy

The Concerned Black Clergy (CBC) was chartered in 1983 with about twenty ministers who were gravely concerned about the condition of homeless people. We thought it was important to address the lack of housing, not simply as it relates to a place to live, but in the sense of creating the notion that adequate housing is a human rights issue. We realized that we had a moral obligation to change the conditions that caused homelessness, not merely furnish beds at night. We began to meet weekly at Paschal's Restaurant. As the number of ministers grew, our concerns expanded beyond homelessness. We have a saying that "the Concerned Black Clergy is not all Black and not all are concerned, but we are effective." In addition to fighting homelessness, we began to speak out against the redlining of neighborhoods, we challenged foreclosures, we supported the Atlanta Food Bank, and we marched against any type of injustice.

Redlining refers to the real estate practice of buying a house in a white neighborhood and selling it to an African-American family. The agents follow up by telling all the whites that the neighborhood is turning Black and their property will quickly decrease in value. These same realtors then buy houses from the whites and sell them to Black people at inflated prices. This practice turns a neighborhood which was predominantly white to predominantly Black. Unfortunately, those who engaged in this practice were acting unjustly to both whites and Blacks. Currently, we're researching the policies of re-gentrification. Because of this strategic, systematic shift by whites back to the city, we say to inner- city Black homeowners, "Keep your home because your property value is going to increase dramatically."

Concerned Black Clergy has also been involved in changing foreclosure practices. The economy has been such that those underemployed, as well as those out of work, cannot make payments on their homes. In the midst of the economic crisis and before, the CBC met with bank presidents and lending agencies to seek relief for people who work hard every day, but simply do not make enough to pay their mortgages. Prior to the job crisis, we focused on getting loans for Black people. When a Black person went into the bank to get a loan for a house, one of the first questions asked was, "What is your address?" If the address was in a predominantly Black section of town, the bank often found a reason not to give the loan. These are the kinds of economic injustices that Concerned Black Clergy will adamantly continue to address.

Of course, Concerned Black Clergy has had a special interest in the differences in educational opportunities on the north side of town, versus the educational opportunities on the south side of town. We believe that there needs to be equity between the two. Concerned Black Clergy has met with public school officials and vehemently expressed dissatisfaction with the vast differences within the same school system. Educational tax dollars should be equally distributed.

In recent years, another primary emphasis has been placed on voter education, voter registration, and getting out the vote. Poor voter registration and participation have been two of the major concerns that the CBC has fought to improve because elected officials directly affect living conditions. We've been strong advocates in the political arena in general. For example, whenever there's an election of a mayor, governor, senator, local official or school board member, we assume an active interest in the outcome. When there are elections, we conduct panels and invite the candidates to share their various political positions. We question them concerning their stances on vital issues that relate to the people we serve. This political awareness and education initiative might not seem to be religious in nature, but it strikes at the root causes of many of the concerns which disenfranchise our community.

When Grady Hospital was preparing to increase the price of prescriptions and change the way they provided care for kidney failure, we immediately staged a protest. We met with the hospital officials at Grady and said, "You cannot increase the prescription costs; you cannot close the renal clinic; you must continue to be a primary source for indigent care." As a result of our protests, Grady kept the cost of prescriptions down, maintained renal care, and is renowned as the best emergency care in the south. The Concerned Black Clergy was in the midst of all of these important discussions and highly credited with being a main source of influence when it comes to speaking out for the less fortunate.

When the city of Atlanta announced plans to ban persons from sleeping on park benches, we saw it as an opportunity to express the need for more homeless shelters. We challenged that ban when we went downtown and slept on park benches too. We protested the city's attitude toward homeless people, because many of them had no place else to sleep. As a result of this protest, there has been an increase in the building of SRO (Single Resident Occupancy) units. Three mayors have made homelessness a part of their platform and administration – Mayors Bill Campbell, Shirley Franklin, and Kasim Reed. They succeeded in the initiative to provide additional sleeping space for Atlanta's homeless population. This proves what can be accomplished when clergy, politicians, and the business community combine their efforts.

The CBC is an active contributor to the Overground Newspaper. We ask each minister who serves in a church to become an "overground conductor," meaning advocate, for the newspaper, which highlights the accomplishments of Black businesses in our community. There are now about 150 businesses in our community that advertise in this newspaper. The newspaper has enlisted about seventy-five ministers who solicit their congregants to shop with the businesses that support the newspaper. The reason we call it the Overground Newspaper is because when 19th-century slaves were escaping to free states, they took the Underground Railroad; naming the newspaper the "Overground" Newspaper offers an homage to that terminology with a more literal meaning related to the accessibility of information to the people. A constant creed and cry of the CBC is, "Let's teach our dollars some cents." So, this newspaper also serves as an economic arm of the Concerned Black Clergy, as we seek to keep hard-earned dollars circulating in our communities. Some research verifies the fact that the African-American dollar circulates only once before it's spent in the broader community. In the Jewish community, the dollar circulates nine times. They understand the necessity to keep their money circulating among themselves, and we decided to emulate that sound economic behavior. We can all learn and prosper when we are open to the positive aspects of what others are doing.

Not long ago, the Atlanta Public School system experienced a cheating scandal, which appeared to implicate a number of Black teachers. Our role as clergypersons was not to challenge whether they were innocent or guilty, but to assure that they were treated fairly. We told the media and others that a few years ago, a major cheating scandal had occurred at Stanford University and also at West Point, but they didn't fire or scandalize the accused professors. They brought in the professors, talked with them and outlined different strategies to achieve their academic goals. Their negotiations cleaned up the concerns. Without the CBC raising our voices in protest, the teachers may not have had a fair opportunity to be heard. The Concerned Black Clergy played an integral part in getting them a fair hearing. When fair and decent-minded people combine their efforts and speak as one voice, justice will prevail.

On another occasion, we stood shoulder to shoulder with about 500 Hispanic school youth who were American citizens, born in this country. They were protesting at the state Capitol building because their parents were being threatened with deportation. We aligned ourselves with them in their right to protest. We wanted to teach them how to protest in a legal way – as we had done in the Civil Rights Movement. For example, we told them that they should not walk in the street without an approved permit, nor block the traffic. They should not do anything that would provoke the police, and avoid at all costs doing anything that would create violence or a confrontation with the police. The protest was conducted in an orderly manner; the students spoke, then together we walked to the World of Coca-Cola. The Concerned Black Clergy fulfilled a role with this immigrant community because we felt that they were being unfairly treated. These are the kinds of actions in which Concerned Black Clergy has and will become involved. We all have a moral responsibility to speak out on behalf of the voiceless in our nation. There is power when we unite.

The Atlanta Business League, which was organized to support

the business efforts of the African-American community, is one of the oldest organizations of its kind. Their goal is to highlight businesses and to offer seminars, workshops, publications, speeches and conferences that improve economic stability in the African-American community. A few years ago, the Atlanta Business League honored a group referred to as "Men of Influence". They highlighted a number of Black men who were successful in their chosen professions. These men of influence were encouraged to reach out to other Black leaders and the larger community to encourage greater spending with African-American owned businesses. For me it was quite an honor to be recognized by this group. Not all honored were businessmen. As a clergyperson, I was inducted as a Man of Influence in 2007. I continue to use my sphere of influence to increase trade among African-American businesses. I intensely believe that I have a calling on my life to enhance the lives and welfare of those whom God allows me to serve. This is my personal creed, and I will abide by it until I die.

The Atlanta Business League also honors "Women of Influence". Outstanding women in our community are chosen and lifted up so that they may be strengthened and encouraged in their work. I've committed my life to breaking down the barriers of ignorance, which separates races, genders, and faiths.

I view my service to the community as in no way separate from my Christian responsibilities and my moral, ethical and justice concerns for people. When I'm speaking about a more enhanced and enriched life in education, economics or improved health, these constitute the basis for a spiritual life pleasing to God. I cannot separate the body, mind and spirit. Whether I'm speaking out against unfair legislation, limiting gun control, limited health care or unjust immigration laws, these are all human issues as well as deep spiritual issues. A pastor's primary function is to, with the help of God, improve the total life of the persons whom he or she is called to serve.

For example, climate change or environmental conditions – it is impossible to separate them from being a moral issue. I don't make distinctions; if something affects persons negatively and disrupts their spiritual growth, that makes it a moral issue. In the Christian community some say, "I'll pick you up, and we'll go to church." That is a false statement because in reality, "the church" is you; "the church" is IN you. It is not a place or a building. You can go to a building and you can go to worship, but you can't "go" to the church. If you say, "I am going to the church," it means when you depart the place, you are leaving the church. You can never leave the church if you are the church. The church must be recognized and accepted as those who are compelled to speak up for the lost and the forgotten. We must tell about good days and better tomorrows.

The Jewish Community Model

In the Jewish community, Judaism is an integral part of their everyday life. They religiously go to the synagogue to worship, which strengthens them in the Jewish faith. What they do, what they think, what they achieve in their lives, and the persons they meet are all respected as a part of the Jewish faith. The Jewish traditions and beliefs are who they are everyday. With respect to Christianity, Christians learn to integrate our religious convictions as a unified part of our very existence. Our faith must constitute who we are and not be an appendage to what we do.

I once attended a bar mitzvah in which an adolescent boy was introduced to manhood; he had to stand before the congregation and demonstrate his personal faith and maturity. He had been rigorously taught the Jewish faith and was proving his worthiness. He had been positively indoctrinated in the Jewish faith. He had to read the Torah in Hebrew and say the prayers in Hebrew. He had to state what he intended to do with his life. This initiation was an integral part of his Jewish religious experience. Having a bar mitzvah marked his becoming a responsible person in our society and an adherent to his faith. Having one's life so ordered has enormous influence on a developing adolescent who learns respect for God, respect for self, and respect for others. It may come as a shock but in the prison population in Georgia, less than one percent is Jewish. I am firmly convinced that the strict teaching of their faith and strong family traditions constitute such an integral code of their being that they fervently refrain from behavior that would bring disgrace to their community.

The church is the ecclesia, those who are set apart to obey God. We are called for a purpose. We are not called out to become a social club or to praise each other, but called out to serve and make God's blessings a reality in the lives of others. So the church as it was conceived was to go into all the world and share the gospel, the message of God's love, to every living creature. It was to reach out to the least, the lost, the left behind and the forgotten. The church is at its peak when it remembers its calling. It is an organism, not an organization, and this organism must be reaching out and transforming life and culture around it for the good of others. These are the mandates given to us by Jesus Christ. We need to ask again, "Who is my neighbor?" When we identify who our neighbor is, we realize that our neighbor needs me to reach out in love, to care for him/her and minister to their needs – to simply be a servant to that person. When the church recognizes, accepts, and believes this, it is more giving. The more it gives, the more it gets and the more it receives from God. The church must go through this cycle of giving and receiving. We must live and survive by what God gives to and through us. To create this kind of life, we must follow our role model, which is found in the life and teachings of Jesus. Jesus said, "It is more blessed to give than to receive." It is a proven fact that, when you give, you receive, so that you may give again. We are to become light in a dark world, signs of hope for the discouraged and depressed. Any member of the Christian faith community who is not deeply concerned and actively engaged in the total welfare of another one of God's human beings is merely a bystander wearing a Christian T-shirt, but not a part of the team!

CHAPTER NINE

✪

I Am Forever Amazed by God's Grace

WHEN I SERVED AS THE DIRECTOR of the Health Promotion Resource Center at the Morehouse School of Medicine, my primary responsibilities included the promotion of health awareness and disease prevention among those with limited healthcare in urban and rural Georgia. I sought to raise the level of awareness among people concerning health hazards, which could save their lives. The program's focus was on healthier diets, increased exercise, reduction of stress, and physical examinations at regular intervals. I was thrilled to be afforded yet another opportunity to be of service. This time it was for physical well-being.

One day, a friend casually asked if I had ever had a colonoscopy. I chuckled and said, "My job is to advise other people about taking care of themselves." I politely let his concern for my personal health pass by, but then I honestly asked myself, "What could it hurt for me to get a colonoscopy?" There are moments when people get so deeply entrenched in their profession that they tend to disregard for themselves the counsel they provide to others. I realize now that I was a perfect illustration of this fault. I decided to call for an appointment and lackadaisically went for my examination. After all, I had no symptoms of illness or pain; therefore, I had no fear of the result of a routine procedure. We learn from ignorance and mistakes if we are honest with ourselves. I was facing a life-changing moment.

Being a Christian minister for the past thirty-five years only reinforced my belief that everything was fine and this medical procedure was merely a time-consuming exercise. I believed that anything I encountered would be overcome by my unyielding, uncompromising faith in God. I felt that I could not lose; if the results came back negative, I would thank and praise God. If the results returned positive, I knew that God could heal anything that ailed me. During my life, if I ever had to face an impossible situation, I knew that my faith could turn impossibilities into possibilities! I recalled that prayer triumphed when I thought my son was dead.

When the results of my test came back, I listened with the utmost confidence and patience as the doctor said, "The results of your examination are inconclusive and to be more definitive in my diagnosis, it will require several additional tests." Those words momentarily penetrated my impenetrable faith. I instantly wondered what a minister who had lived most of his life overcoming insurmountable odds, does when those unexpected, frightening words are spoken, "We have found cancerous polyps."

My initial reaction was, "Is he talking to me about my test results?" I said under my breath, "That's impossible!" I immediately questioned the words "a few more tests will be required." I wondered why. There must have been a misinterpretation of the data because my test results could not possibly indicate polyps that were cancerous. That's impossible. I am the person charged with teaching others about preventive health care; plus, I also pray for the wellness and healing of others. This diagnosis was not mine. Accepting truth is often difficult and can challenge your faith.

More tests – even the thought of subjecting myself to an MRI, CAT scan or ultrasound seemed unimaginable, as well as threatening. I thought to myself, "I won't believe this. I have never been in the hospital for any length of time." I responded like many who face the unknown, "Anything – but CANCER. Not 'the big C.'" I have so much to live for and so many things yet to accomplish. To fully appreciate why I had the unmitigated gall to shout out, "That is impossible," it is necessary to understand who I am and what has compelled me to face challenges and to conquer seemingly overwhelming circumstances.

I was born into a family where my father abruptly abandoned the field of entertainment to become a powerful preacher of the gospel. One day, seemingly for no reason, he changed his lifestyle and expected everyone in the family to do the same. There were three children in our family when our father was convicted, converted, convinced, and committed to the notion that "Nothing is impossible for God." He believed, literally, that if he had faith in God, nothing would be impossible (Matthew 17:20). Thirteen years later, a set of twins and a new daughter increased our family to eight. He believed and drilled into all of us that whatever catastrophe we faced throughout life, nothing was impossible for God; God would guide us safely through. My father constantly told our family that with men and women things may appear impossible, but with God all things are possible (Matthew 19:26). These words formed the core of what I believed then, and I am more certain of their legitimacy today. I continue to use the words of my father to confront all calamities that seek to derail me from accomplishing my goals in life. With God, all things are possible, if you believe.

To comprehend the depth of my belief that nothing is impossible for God, I used it to overcome a severe stuttering problem that held me back in school. This same focused belief system enabled me to become intensely involved in the early days of the Civil Rights Movement while completing college. Graduating from college and being asked to be a member of the first group of U.S. Peace Corps volunteers who were sent to serve in Nigeria, I was startled by God's calling on my life, and my belief that anything was possible was reinforced. Leaving Nigeria, I was recruited to play for the National Basketball Team of Switzerland. Once again, I sensed God's hands directing my young life. I then returned to America and completed a master's degree and a doctorate in psychology. By this time, I was convinced that there was a force governing and guiding my life. I had never planned to be on a national basketball team or go to two graduate schools. I just knew that all of this was possible because of my belief that "Nothing is impossible for God"; yet I continued to feel that my having cancer just wasn't possible. I had lived and played by the rules, but I was now facing the possibility of CANCER. I questioned whether this lifelong belief was true, and whether I was unrealistic in my belief that God was all powerful.

Like most who believe and trust in God, I knew and quoted familiar clichés when faced with this seemingly impossible situation. At one time or another, we have all utilized verbal tidbits to shore up our belief system and to reassure ourselves of God's dominance over our lives. I have used these and other quotes when life's circumstances appeared impossible:

"There is no failure in God."

"God will give you no more than you can bear."

"God is able to subdue all things."

"Nothing is too big for God."

However, when I was finally confronted with the possibility of having cancer, fear invaded my entire belief system, and this fear challenged all of those well-meaning words of faith. Faith – enduring faith – in God's ability to do anything must be tried and tested. Acquiring genuine, pure faith in God is a struggle which we all will encounter during our lifetime.

On that fateful morning, all I heard was, "We need to conduct more tests to determine whether the initial findings of cancerous polyps are valid." My thoughts forced me to imagine being squeezed into and confined in the "casket" of the MRI machine. I felt that I could not do it. It would be impossible. I was deeply afraid of having an MRI, but a friend of mine located an open MRI machine and the fear that I thought was impossible to overcome suddenly became not only possible, but real. When I had completed all of the requested examinations, I was informed that I had colon cancer. My immediate response was that God had not abandoned me. I honestly believed that this was a misdiagnosis. I reasoned that as much as I depended on God, as many pet phrases as I knew, as many sermons as I had preached, as many people as I had comforted, this news was simply impossible in my case. My mind was challenged by this new human reality. This sweeping mental and spiritual tug-of-war reminded me that no one is exempt from having his or her faith tested. I was facing a classic case of doubt and fear, and I knew the Lord.

What surprised me at the doctor's final, official pronouncement of my health condition was that what I initially thought was impossible was now a fact. My denial of having cancer was shattered. It was a fact! I had cancer. All of my rationalizing of why this was impossible was washed away. I ate right and exercised regularly. I am a faithful husband, a good father, and a Christian minister – all of that clamored in my head. I was shocked as to why God would allow the sentence of death to be my epitaph. When cancer was mentioned, it ignited a spiritual response that forced me to once again rely on my frequently quoted spiritual clichés, proven Scriptures, and prayers. I had to cling on to them for survival. I had to face the medical truth that I had cancer, and now I had to believe that nothing is impossible with God. I was flunking the faith test.

For me to accept this news was a real challenge, and I questioned my readiness to move forward with trusting God or the medical profession. Do the two work hand in hand? I continued to create in my mind a death sentence. They informed me that extensive chemotherapy treatments would probably be necessary. A person taking chemotherapy would contend with physical tiredness and multiple unimaginable side effects. How could God allow this to happen? It still just seemed impossible. The dreaded dooming effect of doubt began to consume my thoughts. I secretly questioned whether God would use some "impossible medical finding" and cure me. Maybe for the first time, I honestly sought God's counsel, comfort, and guidance. I questioned why I waited so long to trust God. From then on, my faith in God's ability to honor his healing promises began to develop, and my acceptance that the doctors knew more than I did became real. However, I now knew for myself that I serve a sovereign God who had never, ever failed me. What a searing recognition! I was liberated.

Laparoscopic surgery was performed, and the diseased section of the colon was removed. What I feared was impossible – my acquiring the disease and then being cured – became possible. I can attest now, more than ever before, that those biblical words that encourage us to trust in God must become an integral part of our lives, and when crises occur, facing the truth is the first step we are driven to take. I've never doubted or questioned whether the Godhead, the omnipotent power, could cure me; however, I did question whether it was His will to do it.

I reasoned that His will and my desire might not be in harmony. But I remembered the verse, "By his stripes we are healed." What does that really mean? It means that no weapon, not even cancer, formed against me can win. I needed these words of wisdom to encourage my faith. LISTEN—THEY WORK.

Deep down inside I could not shake the feeling that my undesired medical report was now possible. I played by the rules, obeying God's directives, and I treated neighbors and foes with dignity, so how could God permit cancer to inhabit my body? These damaged feelings of God's unfaithfulness brought on tinges of disappointment, frustration, and maybe a little anger. In the midst of these extremely compelling emotions to surrender my fate to God, I recalled another scripture that came from the lips of Jesus: "Let this cup pass from me." I asked myself why I should be excluded from drinking from this cup of cancer. I found my comfort and peace when I remembered the words, "Father, into your hands I surrender my spirit, my will, and my future. Have your way with me." When these words became a reality in my spirit, I finally had a sense of absolute peace. The bottom line to this internal, spiritual war was to surrender completely to God's purpose for my life, and trust that He knows best.

I was then engulfed in an atmosphere that assured me that everything was in divine order. The centerpiece of trust allowed me to accept my condition, and the familiar clichés now had new meaning. I began this new, exciting, liberating, faith- empowered journey with optimistic fervor. The surgery was successful. We all celebrated, until I was confronted with the news that there was a need for a preventive procedure – ten months of chemotherapy was recommended. My question was, "Why, if you got all of the cancer?" My first realization was that the operation was not as successful as I had been led to believe. Hence, chemotherapy would be required. Just for a fleeting moment, I had feelings of acute anxiety which seemed to control my restored faith. I was, once again, forced to believe in my father's original exhortations that nothing was impossible for God – even curing my cancer.

The doctor instructed me that I would be taking chemotherapy every Monday. I knew that such treatments were in the best interest of my long-term health, and I reluctantly joined my new chemotherapy family and took my assigned weekly chemotherapy chair. I quickly realized that the time required for the treatments limited my normal, extremely busy schedule. I realized that God has an uncanny way of using prescribed treatments to create new vistas of understanding by placing us with those who appear to be in worse condition than ourselves. I was introduced to those who sat next to me during our treatments and ignorantly surmised that those who knew me might have been questioning my faith in God since they saw me as medically needy as they were. This was faulty thinking on my part. Soon my chemotherapy family began to pray with and for each other, and a mutual admiration society was born. We shared stories of fear, doubt, joy, laughter, losses, victories, tears, pain, and hope. Each personal revelation was a source of strength for each of us. After a few months, our clinicians became part of our support family too, and a truly healing environment was created to meet whatever need was present. I learned that regardless of our heavenly dependence on God, we all need each other here on earth.

A lesson was reinforced for me, which I will forever cherish: "God uses other people to bring blessings into our lives." I remember the first time I heard that statement on a cold, frozen street in Washington D.C., when Dr. Lawrence Neil Jones, the Dean of the Howard Divinity School, spoke them to me. We must be open and willing to receive whomever and whatever God sends into our lives by abandoning our doubts, fears, and feelings of hopelessness which will destroy us. I now acknowledge the fact that, even though I am a person of faith and a pastor, I am neither perfect nor invincible; I don't have to be more holy than others – I'm human, too!

Eventually, the smell of the medicine during the chemotherapy, which occasionally upset my stomach, became a fragrance of love, support, companionship and genuine caring. I began to smile each week and entered the clinic with the anticipation of seeing how God would unfold new possibilities for joy during our treatment time together. The cleaning of the port, waiting for the blood count, and the injection of the medicine, all became a meaningful part of God's divine plan for my life. Chemotherapy did not become any easier, nor did I look forward to it, but each treatment increased my faith in God. Yes, question God's will and His divine purpose for your life, but when it is revealed to you, be patient with yourself and The Almighty.

Regardless of the catastrophic news we may receive, no one is exempt from abrupt changes in life. Our response to what appears to be life-threatening or life-ending is most critical. To deny what you know is happening is a little naïve, because disastrous events can happen to any one of us at any time. Honestly seek to understand what God is doing. Here's an interesting acknowledgment—seemingly, the more intelligent we are, the more we depend on ourselves and the less we depend on God.

Events and circumstances do not happen because we are good, bad, indifferent, rich, poor or in the wrong place. It is paramount to remember that rather than allowing life-altering events to awaken subliminal doubt and lead to questions like "why me?" or "what did I do to deserve this?," we must tenaciously grasp our faith and trust in God. To awaken our faith, we must realize that God is ultimately in charge and will render the final results. Know and believe that nothing is impossible for God and that what may appear to be disastrous may actually be a challenge for personal and spiritual development. God created you and knows you far better than you know yourself.

When a situation seems impossible and the answers to our questions leave us full of doubt, when the words "nothing is impossible with God" may have lost their significance, that's when we must stop and refocus our faith. I finally found my peace and assurance when I heard the words, "when cancer returns, it comes with a vengeance." Deep down inside, I immediately rejected those words. I knew that the return of cancer was possible, but those threatening words had been muffled because I knew that since God healed me once, He could do it again. True faith is when you live each day to its fullest knowing that whatever happens, God is in total control. Relax and enjoy the life God has provided for you.

During those spiritually enriching and empowering months, I became more understanding and accepting of my humanity. My appreciation of what can unexpectedly transpire to alter one's course in life had been enhanced. When I was forced to admit that cancer had become a resident in my body, it did not mean that cancer would be a permanent one. Tragedy is a visitor in all of our lives, and there are lessons to be learned during these special times of testing. I learned that once cancer has been diagnosed, it should not be an all-consuming way of life. Cancer is merely a comma in the sentence of life, not necessarily a period.

I want to report to those who read these words of inspiration, comfort, and guidance, what has come to me from my two years of battling cancer. The fear of cancer has greatly improved my prayer life. This journey has opened my mind and spirit to broader visions of service. My family, friends, and church members are cherished even more. I view them from a different perspective. Persistently I have wondered if they understand or agree with my view of life and God's power, when I say that everything is possible with and for God.

When one properly prepares to travel the long and winding road of cancer, it can be life-enriching and meaning-filled with magical possibilities. Cancer, when put in the appropriate context, can teach us a lesson about living. I do believe the promise that "nothing is impossible with God!" Whatever we may see as impossible, for whatever reason, God has an answer. If the diagnosis of cancer comes to you or your family, rather than saying, "That is impossible," regard it as yet another opportunity to remember the sufficiency of God. Every day, every event, every moment, every encounter is just another kairos moment for God to stretch your faith. Are you ready to have your faith tested?

Kenya's and Muriel's Bouts with Cancer

Normally, Muriel gets up in the morning before I do; she is always busy around the house most of the day and has more energy than most anyone I know. On this particular day, I got up before her. I thought it strange, but people do get tired. Later that day, when I got home, I discovered that she had been lying on the couch all day. I suggested that we go upstairs and get in the bed. She slowly got up and climbed the steps to our bedroom. I turned the lights off downstairs and quickly followed her upstairs. She was in the bathroom washing her face when I heard this loud crash. I dashed into the bathroom and there she was, lying on the floor with her eyes rolled back; her head had hit the shower door and shattered it. Her body looked lifeless. I thought she was dead.

When I felt Muriel's body, she was burning up with fever. I took her in my arms, lifted her head, and fervently splashed water all over her; when I finished, we both were thoroughly soaked. I wondered why and how she had fallen and what caused her body to be so hot. I reasoned that maybe she stumbled or tripped on the bathroom rug and hit her head on the shower door. Or maybe she fainted. In addition to these two symptoms, she had broken out with a rash which covered her entire body. I decided not to call the doctor that night after she seemed to come around. Finally, I got her cooled down. After her temperature decreased, we dried off and went to bed. I did not sleep at all; instead I prayed once again for understanding and the acceptance of God's will.

The next day we went to the doctor to see about the fainting, the fever and the spots on her body; the horrible spots on her made her skin appear to look like alligator skin. We thought maybe she had a rash or was allergic to a vaccination. First we went to see a dermatologist; when she finished the examination, she said that she needed some more tests. At first she thought Muriel had shingles and insisted that the blood test would help her determine what was going on in her body. Not knowing what she was experiencing made Muriel very anxious.

The doctor then asked me what hospital I preferred because she needed to get Muriel admitted. I called Dr. Tookes, a friend of mine, and he admitted her to Piedmont Hospital. They placed her in a quarantine room, but the doctors still had no idea what was causing her condition. She remained in the hospital for ten days while the specialists were trying to diagnose what was transpiring. During the time that she was in the quarantine room, no one could visit her but me. I was supposed to wear a gown and a mask when I entered the room, but I couldn't. I couldn't force myself to cover up with a hospital gown and mask appearing to isolate myself from her or make her feel any worse.

I wasn't afraid to risk catching whatever was in the room if it meant being with my wife. Later, I was informed that the gown and mask were to protect her from possible outside germs. Faulty perceptions can be highly deceptive.

After performing a number of tests and evaluating the results, the doctors diagnosed her with chronic lymphatic leukemia. Her white blood cell count was 250,000 when a normal count is about 9,000. Months later, Muriel's test showed that her white blood count was 3,600. The doctors questioned Muriel further about whether she'd had chickenpox since they originally thought she also had shingles. They were trying to diagnose the additional illness as chickenpox or shingles because her immune system was so low. She was vulnerable to any disease she encountered, and her immune system was sending warning signals. Under these conditions, an accurate diagnosis was very difficult. Whatever disease was present, her body had no resistance to it. In the church, for example, she could have likely encountered someone who had chickenpox and her body took on the symptoms of this disease. If the disease that invaded her system had been more serious than chickenpox, it could have been fatal. Fortunately, none of these worst case scenarios occurred; they were able to treat the chickenpox symptoms and accurately isolate the leukemia. It is hard to believe that when the diagnosis was confirmed, I felt blessed. "God has spoken . . . let the church say AMEN!"

When Muriel got the cancer diagnosis, the doctor said that when she began chemo, she would definitely lose her hair. He also acknowledged the obvious, that every woman has a problem with hair loss. Because we were expecting Muriel to lose her hair, she and our daughter went out and purchased two beautiful wigs. Oddly, Muriel didn't lose her hair and she has never worn even one of those wigs. I wish she had kept the receipts, so we could return those unused wigs and get our money back. They are still in the closet. Only God controls the hair on our head, or the lack thereof. Trust God.

Muriel and I were not the only people in our family to have cancer. Our daughter-in-law, Hasan's wife, Kenya, also had a bout with second stage breast cancer. Our granddaughter was performing in an activity at school, and we were in attendance. In the course of their conversation Muriel asked Kenya how she had been getting along. She immediately responded that she had found a lump in her breast. Muriel said, "You need to talk with a doctor immediately." Kenya followed up with an appointment. After an examination the doctor told her that she had second stage breast cancer; the higher the number, the more serious the cancer, so this was serious but not untreatable. At the same time, her mother was recovering from breast cancer; I wondered if perhaps there is a genetic connection regarding some types of cancer. Knowing that her mother was suffering from breast cancer likely influenced Kenya's self-examination and her mentioning the lump to Muriel. She came through all the treatments just fine and today is cancer free. Our family has been visited with cancer: between Kenya, me and Muriel, we had a cancer club in our family. This illness proved to be a blessing in that we trusted God even more and depended on one another on a daily basis. Our children and grandchildren saw faith and love in action.

When this illness came to Kenya, she couldn't work. At the time Hasan was not working, and their savings were rapidly dissolving. Through this illness though, they learned their true source for survival. Their dependence on knowing that all things are possible with God secured their love and marriage.

Acknowledging and dealing with cancer has been difficult, but as a consequence, we are a closer family. All of us have reached out to others who have a special need. Whoever is suffering, whoever has a problem, receives our attention. This responsiveness has been good for our family because it is hard to think about yourself when you're thinking about other people and their health. Since we have all recovered from cancer, two Sundays each month we share Sunday dinners that involve Muriel and me, our children and grandchildren. On these Sundays when we come together, we ban cell phones and iPads and any other electronic distractions to our family conversation. With a high degree of intentionality we build up our family with a good meal and intimate time together. The strength of an enduring family is to face, endure, and overcome any perceived setbacks, and to celebrate the joy of living.

Muriel and I have become more focused on our grandchildren and their activities. Rewarding their achievements and supporting them in their chosen activities has become important to us. Our grandson and granddaughter are champion swimmers. This sport is usually viewed as a "white person's sport", but in spite of this false expectation, our grandchildren are excellent swimmers. Our other granddaughter is a scholar and a basketball player, and our oldest grandson received a four-year scholarship to the Naval Academy. I am truly grateful for what has happened in our family as a consequence of battling cancer. I have never heard anyone complain about winning the lottery, but people generally complain about a cancer diagnosis. When people win the lottery, they celebrate; but when something like cancer occurs, celebrations and thankfulness to God are far away. As believers, we should learn to thank God for the highs and the lows, the good and the bad. Praise God simply for never abandoning you, whatever the diagnosis.

Muriel would definitely say that cancer has affected her spiritually. It has made her realize even more that she is totally dependent upon God. Through her whole illness she believed that she was going to be healed. And she has been. She cannot say that she is completely cancer free, because she will live with it in her system for a while longer. But she has been cured to a degree that she feels well and has an excellent quality of life.

One day, after the cancer was mostly conquered, I heard Muriel say, "I think having cancer caused me to realize that I'm not in charge of my life. I've always known that God has been in charge of my life, but this experience with cancer has made my faith more definite, more concrete. All the positive beliefs that I have had and all the hope that is promised us by God, I now am living. My faith today is more solid and that's a good thing, because I can now pass it on to my children and my grandchildren with confidence."

When both Muriel and I were living with cancer, we realized how much our church family cared for and served us. Going through the uncertainty, taking the treatments and feeling our church family shower us with love, made life so much more bearable. When we faced these tests of faith, it was wonderful to know that there were people around us who held us up. Never choose to go through any crisis alone. Find someone who genuinely cares and face the ordeal together under God's grace and mercy.

We have also witnessed our daughter-in-law draw closer to God. Whenever she speaks of her healing and her cure, she gives God credit. She also demonstrates a desire for her children, our grandchildren, to realize that everything comes to us from God, rather than from our own efforts. I now believe that all of us are on the right track; God used our cancer to show us a deeper way of sharing and loving. God is always seeking to bring us closer to Him and thus is an integral part in all we experience. Seek God's intervening power in whatever you may encounter. God's divine presence is just below the surface.

We are proud of our son, the man he has become and the father that he is to our grandchildren. When Kenya was ill, he took care of our granddaughter and grandson. One day I asked him, "Do you realize how few men have the opportunity to learn how to braid their daughter's hair?" Kenya's being ill gave him that opportunity. I know now that when a father braids the hair of his daughter, a different kind of bond begins to exist between them.

This entire ordeal has really made me rethink what's really important in my life and commitments. Did I do all that I could do with the people I know, the places I've been, and through the experiences I've had? Did I do everything I could have done for them? Have I done the best I could do for Muriel, showing her the appreciation I have for her and the life we share? In this regard, many of my colleagues took a different route: they got a job, they worked hard, they saved their money, they built a substantial retirement, and now they are retired and enjoying life with their families. What am I doing? I'm still meeting with committees! I'm still serving on boards! I'm still preaching, pastoring and conducting retreats! Am I being smart? How do I take all the gifts God has given me, maximize them and do something for Muriel? The time has arrived for my personal life assessment. Redirection, not retirement; refocusing, not retirement; recommitment… NOT retirement.

A Few Admonitions

We all face challenges and struggles through life. Some may appear overwhelming; others may not be quite so disturbing. It is important for us to understand that no matter what happens in our life, it doesn't happen to us, it happens for us. In my case, I had to understand that no matter what happened in my life, it didn't happen TO me, but FOR me. Whatever you are going through, whatever situation you face, no matter how high the mountain or how deep the valley, there is an answer to the question, "Why me?" The answer may not be what you want it to be; the first solution may not be the final solution, but it all completes a composite picture of your life. What we most deeply desire is a sense of wholeness, a sense of completion, an understanding that life continues no matter what the circumstances. In life, we may never get the solution that we want, but we will get what is best for us. Remember, the journey in seeking the answer is just as important as the solution. You finally understand life when you know that each adventure, circumstance and condition is a moment to be blessed.

When something comes into your life, do not deny that it is happening. Look at what is really going on with you, and learn to accept it. If you can change it—change it. Life is like sandpaper. It can smooth out the rough places. Sandpaper can be rough, sandpaper can scratch, but sandpaper can smooth out the jagged edges – that is what makes it so valuable to furniture makers as well as life-makers. Tragedies or accidents or catastrophes or whatever may come, work like sandpaper to smooth out our lives. Whatever happens to you also happens for you because it helps you discover that life is sometimes tough. It shows you that you cannot manage life on your own. Though we have great doctors, great pastors, great psychologists and great teachers – there's a time in all our lives when unforeseen events occur. Don't deny what's going on with you and don't be afraid to recognize your moment to grow. Allow someone to help you help yourself. Nobody can carry you, but they can put an arm around you and walk with you through the rough places in life.

Keep a certain sense of levity about life. God gives us a sense of humor to confront any situation. Don't beat yourself up! There are plenty of things in life to beat you down. So don't beat yourself up. Your overall goal is to reach a degree of completeness in your life, to feel whole. Not everything goes according to your plans, but it is important to live with a sense of confidence. When you look toward the future, you must also look at the present knowing that you have the power and the strength to succeed in your future. You must be able to say, "I know that I will make it. I can get through this ordeal." You may be wandering in the desert, but you can say, "I know there's water close by." The psychological, physiological, and spiritual all come together to give you a sense of completeness and wholeness. The way of peace and wholeness has been built into you and me. We can count on it. This is the way that life is.

I believe there are forces that can help you. Don't quit, don't turn around, and don't give up! Don't yield to negativity. Always keep a positive faith. I don't mean a Pollyanna faith, but believe and trust and expect a miracle from God. Be still; be quiet until you can receive a period of deep spiritual meditation. Meditation has a healing, empowering, transformational effect in our life. In times of stress, go inside of yourself and draw on that inner reservoir of strength that is in you! Sometimes you can't find anything inside of you, but it is there. Return again and again until you can draw on it for strength to get to the next positive level. There is always a next level. There is a well of peace within each of us that overflows with joy and gratitude.

As Jimmy Valvano so memorably said, "Don't give up! Don't ever give up!" This is your time to be amazed at who you are and what you have accomplished thus far with your God-inspired and empowered life. Experience the feeling of "being amazed." It's truly a liberating feeling!

CHAPTER TEN

✪

I Am Amazed at the Power of God's Word

THERE IS SOMETHING CONVINCING about those who are called to preach. The Bible says, "Many are called, but few are chosen". I sometimes wonder today if many are preaching who have not been called. I listen to quite a number of preachers today that I think maybe received a call from Verizon, AT&T, or Sprint, but not from God. I don't know if they were called by God, which is not my judgment to make. Some seem to have been called by necessity, called because they lost a job or because they can sing a little better than others. I believe that an authentic calling of God to preach comes from a deep conviction down inside, one that compels a person to become actively engaged in improving the well-being of others. Truly called men and women encounter a compelling force within themselves that drives them to make a difference in other people's lives; I am referring to the tangible, visible aspects of God's presence in work, family, justice and service.

In order for a difference to be made in people's lives, they must encounter change. In order for them to change internally, they must find a power greater than their own. If the preacher has a gift for leading, he or she can effectively introduce people to that amazing power in the human spirit, that power I call God! This power creates a new being on the inside, and that manifests itself on the outside. We who speak for God are merely voices that point other people to a power greater than themselves. So the words coming out of the preacher's mouth must convince listeners to turn toward God and to find an inner strength that enables them to live a more peaceful and faithful life. People who listen to God and walk in His ways may even find something greater than preaching and faith in the future. They find the complete assurance of God's matchless love. Our task today is to help people while they are alive to find solutions for their daily problems and hope for their tomorrows. Our aim is to lift the burden, relieve the anxiety and undergird them with new possible visions for the future.

The message that we proclaim is not our message but God's message; if it is only our message, it will not have the power to transform. We have two ancient writings which we refer to as the Old Testament and the New Testament. We who speak for God search the words, sayings and truths of these holy books so that our words reflect what God desires us to share. God's exhortations are not limited to the Bible or Bible times; they speak inspiringly to us here and now. The task of the preacher is to find a text or a thought or an idea that on Sunday morning will help Aunt Sally find a reason to get up on Monday morning. The worship time must give her strength to live through the tests and trials of the week.

I've been allowed to share spiritual thoughts with people of all economic levels who are struggling with life, and I've found that the same truth applies to these persons as it applies to the chairman of the board of directors, to the president of a company, or to the president of the United States. Every one of us, whether we are rich or poor, Black or white, needs the enriching, empowering presence of God in our lives. Human thoughts and inspirations lead us, but God-inspired guidance empowers us. Without spirit there is no positive energy.

When ministers desire to speak to the people on Sunday morning, their task is to take what they believe theologically and state it in a manner that it speaks to people's daily lifestyles. If it does not inspire today, it is useless; it is only masquerading as truth. In the seminary, we learn theological and biblical truths that should become our message. When we preach in a parish, we learn practicality, which is what our members need every day of their lives – practical teaching. If God's word is not practical for relieving the daily pressures of life, then its meaning is useless.

Everything in the worship service should lead hearts and minds to the inspired spoken Word of God. The Word of God may be sung; it may be recited in testimony; it can be heard in the music; it also oozes out of the lives of believers; and specifically, the Word of God can be heard through the words of Scripture when we open our hearts to it. All of these different aspects of a worship service lead to the preached word which should give hope for a more productive life now and relieve any anxiety.

Words properly spoken are powerful! Words constitute the end product of our thought. What we think about comes out in the form of words; words tend to direct our behavior. Negative words create a destructive force field around us. Positive words create a positive, imaginative atmosphere around us. We who are in the preaching ministry are constantly using words to communicate the Spirit of God to people. In preaching we attempt to communicate a lifestyle that is meaningful and fulfilling.

Jesus used words to tell stories and called them parables. You never know how your words impact other people. When a preacher rises to preach, he/she may receive the Amens, Praise the Lords, and Hallelujahs, but it is quite a tribute when someone in your congregation writes down the words that are being said. Words and phrases that impact them find their way onto a page where they are reviewed over and over by that member of the congregation. Those words are agents of change. Of course, when you're standing there preaching, you're not thinking about people writing down notes and packing them away for another day. At that moment a preacher is endeavoring to be the spokesperson for God. There's no room for selfish or self-serving thoughts. People know when the preacher "sits down" and God "stands up." People from all cultures recognize God's voice.

Testimonials are critical for the worship experience. For example, when a woman stands to tell her story, she is enabling other members to hear and see what God is doing in a human life. When she tells her story about cancer, she emphasizes how God picked her up out of the bed and put her feet on the floor. She testifies to how the strength of God gave her energy to walk again and to live through His grace. When she is telling her story, there may be eight or eighty people sitting behind or before her who need to hear her assuring words of witness. They may be confused about their own lives, but they are sitting in the pews listening, waiting expectantly to hear God speak through testimony and preaching. So preaching is a means to help individual people find and understand their own experience with God, and through that experience to see life through different eyes, eyes that have been opened by the miracle of the preached word.

When Jesus met the woman at the well, He did not say, "One day you shall get water." No, He gave her water from the well that day; she went back to town with spiritual water inside her. When Jesus was hanging on the cross, He did not say to the thief, "I'll see you someday." No! He said, "Today you will be with me in paradise." People sitting in the pews need to hear a word from God today, not tomorrow, not next year, but now!

I believe that people hear the Word of God when the preacher is anointed by God. This anointing comes alive in the preacher and is transmitted to those before him/her in worship. The message should stand above and far beyond the preacher; it is more profound than the preacher. The Spirit within God's messenger and within the atmosphere of worship makes the preacher's spoken words become the Word of God to the listeners. The preacher does not have this power at his/her command, but is daily dependent upon God to be revealed to the preacher and through the preacher. This does not mean that the preacher is free from being prepared to preach, but when speaking, there is dependency upon the Spirit of God to take those fragile human words and translate them into the Word of God. Sometimes, though, when the preacher has had extensive preparation, fresh images, ideas and illustrations reveal themselves during the preaching moment in a way not thought about before. This sudden inspiration is the work of God in the mind and soul of the preacher. When Jesus set this preaching in motion, He chose fishermen, tax collectors, farmers, and ordinary people to be proclaimers of His message. God empowered them through their experience of the Living Jesus Christ to speak to average ordinary people about the love and presence of God. Without a doubt people heard God speak to their hearts, and because they believed, they were changed.

We can truthfully say to people today, "You need not worry. Worry is disbelief; worry is not trusting in God." We have the promise of God that He has not given us "the spirit of fear but of power, of love, and of a sound mind." (II Timothy 1:7) God places in our hearts His divine love for us so that we are thus made steady and strong to approach any of the tasks He gives us. When people hear this philosophy, many say, "I must stop worrying and trust God; I will trust and obey the God who loves me." We also sing this Word, "Hold to God's unchanging hand." The song goes like this: "Time is filled with swift transition, naught of earth unmoved can stand, build your hopes on things eternal, hold to God's unchanging hand." I say to people, "Don't hold to my hand; I may fail you. Hold to God's unchanging hand!" Never forget that you and God are the majority.

I have been surrounded in the congregation by people who have heard God speak to them and who believe that He has faithfully brought them through the fiery trials of life. A few years ago I met a man in the congregation who said to me, "I believe I have finally heard what you're saying." He then began reflecting on what I had said and what he had heard. He said, "I believe that now I understand God's basic message." Flesh and blood did not reveal this to him; it was the Holy Spirit at work in his mind taking the words he had heard and making them the Word of God in his heart. To hear what purpose God has for your life, you must be openly receptive and believe that God knows and loves you.

With all my heart, I believe my grandmother was in constant communication withGod. She did not go to formal worship, but she gave me pearls of wisdom that have stayed with me for over seventy years. God spoke through her to me, and at the time, she had no idea that she was being the spokesperson for God. I didn't consciously connect with God in those years either, yet today I realize that she was sharing with me what God wanted me to know. She taught me about life in the real world; she taught me the virtue of honesty; she taught me how to humble myself and how to view people with sincere appreciation. Today when I see God in people, I recognize them as people of humility. These humble people don't need to impress me or anyone else. God-empowered people never need to impress others.

A few of the people who have spoken the Word of God to me would be really shocked to hear me say that God had spoken through them. Yet, the transmission of God's Word happens every day through scores of people who are not aware of how they are instruments of God. I recall people in my life like Coach Howdy Green, who taught me some of life's great lessons. I doubt that he realized he was speaking God's Word to me. But Coach Green taught me not to be a thug. To be considerate and compassionate while caring for others was his creed. Are these not words from God?

Every now and then, a tough lesson was taught to me. I was sitting in the locker room at Tennessee State University with my cap on my head. Coach Green came by and slapped my hat off my head. This infuriated me. I said to myself, I'm the double, defensive, delectable, darling, dynamic, dangerous, devastating D from Denver ("Double-D" was my high school nickname). I was filled with rage because he slapped my hat off. I put the hat back on and he slapped it off again. He did it a third time without flinching or changing his posture or attitude. He must not have known that I was the Double-D from Denver because nobody puts his hand on the Double-D's hat. He told me, "I don't know you, I don't care a thing about you, but I want you to learn to be a gentleman. If you are to be a gentleman, you must learn that you don't wear your hat inside the house."

"Furthermore," he said, "If you put the hat back on your head, I'm going to slap it back off." I walked back to the dorm after that encounter as angry as I could be, but as I look back over that moment, he was right. He gave me a lesson in humility and made me think about who I truly was, and what I needed to become and do to be successful in life. The Word of God does that, whether spoken by a preacher or a layperson. This encounter was as painful to me as the one with Sam Proctor, who asked me those three embarrassing questions in front of Sargent Shriver. But in both instances I was taught something that I needed to know. Sometimes the Word of God comes to us in very rough packages, packages we had just as soon throw away. Yet, never forget that some real jewels come in rough packages. Diamonds are first lumps of coal, but time creates a valuable gem. A piece of sand in an oyster shell becomes a pearl. Gold becomes purer in fire. Lessons are learned through struggles.

Recalling this conversation with Coach Green makes me think of my relationship with my father. When I was growing up, I thought that he was terribly tough on me, giving me very little time or attention, so I distanced myself from him. Today I realize what he was trying to do with and for me. I understand now how burdened with life he was and what he had to do when he was seventeen or eighteen. He had two sons, a daughter and a wife to feed and later he had three more children. He always held down two jobs; he preached in the church and sold Nutrilite Vitamins and other items to get enough money for the family to live on. He was so busy and always gone back then, but I've since learned to deeply appreciate his sacrifice, and what it means to sacrifice for others. When one understands the concept of sacrificial love, then certain acts can no longer be considered selfish or self-centered.

Words of Wisdom

When you are in the pulpit, breaking the bread of life, you never know what those sitting before you are thinking. When I am preaching, quite often cryptic sayings and witticisms come into my mind and flow out through my mouth. These words are seldom in my notes. While these inspired words may not be in my manuscript, I believe they are God-infused in that moment. I always tell people that when they go to worship, to open their hearts and ears because God has brought them there for a specific purpose. When people open their hearts, they will hear what God has to say to them that day for their own personal and spiritual development. People who go to worship expecting nothing, get exactly that – NOTHING!

To illustrate that people who do come to worship with an open mind and open heart will receive the Word of God, I want to describe a certain member of the congregation. Some years ago a lady, who for some time had been a member of Providence Church, told me that she was moving to California. One Sunday morning she came and spoke with me in my office. She pensively said, "Before I leave for California, let me tell you what your ministry has meant to me." Then she patiently said that many of the phrases, thoughts, and ideas that she had heard in my sermons were very important to her life. She said, "I have summarized what I derived from your sermons and made a list of your phrases." She then said that she would like to share these quotations with me. She handed me a sheet of paper with her notes from numerous sermons on it. As I quickly read through the list, I was amazed at how deeply I agreed with what I was reading. I had no difficulty agreeing with what I had previously preached; I just didn't remember preaching it. As I read her notes, I found words that I recalled saying, but I couldn't tell when or in what context I said them. This wonderful woman gave this treasure to me and I can't even recall her name, but I do remember my feelings of delight as I read through the list. There are those lives that you touch that you are totally unaware of. That's when you understand that God is speaking through you.

I was deeply surprised that I had said something that this woman thought was worth remembering. In a situation where I am affirmed, I usually feel somewhat embarrassed. I laugh and nod my head and then shake it off, pretending it never happened. I don't think that this is the best response. I wish that I could let people tell me that they appreciate me without explaining away their deep feelings of appreciation and love.

As I thought about what this woman had done in clinging to these words of wisdom for her life, I said, "I want to thank you for what you have offered me today." An unexpected experience like this made me realize that when I talk about what is going on in my life, it usually also applies to someone else. This gift also reassured me that the ministry I have had was meaningful to someone and maybe does last beyond the Sunday morning worship service. After reading over her list of my sayings, I shared the quotations with my wife, Muriel. As she read them, she said, "I remember when you said that. Yes, I remember this other saying too." Muriel concluded with this: "Jerry, this woman has really captured you in these quotations."

I want to share with you the list she provided me, and I pray that one or two will be a blessing to you.

Circumstances don't give me joy. They give me opportunities.

The praise team shouldn't have to pump us up.

When you are having hard times, it is a sign that you are a threat to the enemy.

Pray and ask God, "What are my gifts?"

When you are inside a storm, do not allow the storm to get inside of you.

You cannot have a padlock on your stuff and beg from God.

Hold your peace in times of trouble.

Know God is in control, even in your darkest hour.

Satan fights the hardest when God has something in store for you.

Don't let the news media steal your joy.

God is not the digger of the depression pit.

You can't stand on sand.

Preachers need love and people to love them too.

You don't come to church to get entertained.

Do you want to be a mega-church or a mega-mission church?

You know, I played some mean ball.

Just because you have your GED, you think you don't need a GOD.

Like sheep, we nibble until we stray.

Let God be God.

Know that God is blessing you right now.

Don't try to figure it out; let God take over.

It is not your job to run the world.

God guarantees peace.

Traveling light means trusting God with the burdens
you were never intended to bear.

Who is your shepherd?

Be careful who you call your enemy.

God does not intend for you to carry shame.

God doesn't need your two dollars.

If you can't define the problem, you can't solve it.

There is nothing worse than an insecure Christian.

Hold on to the blessing, not the circumstance.

When you can't sleep at night, don't grab Sominex, grab Sermonex.

Do not let religiosity destroy your connection to an Almighty and
Sovereign God.

Never sell yourself short.

We are the work of the Master Crafter.

God is not the author of confusion or pity parties.

Hell is when you meet the person you could have been.

The source of success is often naïveté and humility.

Reflections from My Sermons

Another amazing thing happened to me one Sunday after service. A member of the church came forward and gave me a framed placard with quotes from sermons I had preached over the past several years. The member was the chief of a native tribe from Nigeria. Here's his story.

Chief Tunde Adetunji was from Nigeria. He was a chief, who at one time worked for Swissair. Swissair was seeking to create a base in Nigeria; they chose Chief Tunde Adetunji to guide them in the cultural mix and the manner in which they had to function to make their efforts successful. He helped with the training of the Swissair employees in Africa. He was well respected and highly sought after as a gifted communicator and trainer.

After a few years they moved him to Switzerland, where he continued the training of Swissair employees. Chief Tunde Adetunji trained airline employees how to work with people on the continent of Africa. Very soon he realized that Swissair was using him; they were elevating everyone else, but overlooked him at promotion time. In addition to teaching them the African culture, he was teaching them about the art of Africa. Unfortunately, the company had very little interest in his passion for art. Swissair was interested in business, in opening up Lagos and the western side of the continent. When they seemed not to share his interest in art, he spoke with the management and emphasized to them that to understand the environment, they had to appreciate Africa's heritage and culture.

When Swissair executives seemed uninterested, he decided to immigrate to the United States and make Atlanta, Georgia his home.

Chief Tunde Adetunji had one of the largest African art collections in the world. He decided to bring all of his art to Atlanta and open the African Art Museum and put his artifacts on display. Some of the most expensive paintings and clearest examples of African ingenuity were in his collection. He used this valuable collection to open a museum of African history and art. About the time he opened the African Museum, I was one of those personally invited to his exposition. Needless to say, I was deeply moved and became a devotee to the chief.

As we were walking through the museum, I had a positive impression of Chief Tunde Adetunji. He told me that his goal was to use the museum as a way of bringing African-Americans in touch with their heritage. He was a very spiritual man. He wanted me to introduce him to the mayor so that he could attract his attention and interest him in this worthwhile project. Already he was entertaining a variety of people by giving African art and cultural presentations.

He was bringing in important people to Atlanta from many African countries, like Ghana, Kenya, South Africa and Nigeria. I was always asked to be one of his presenters because I was an African-American pastor living in Atlanta. This introduction eventually led to my meeting his wife and his children. After a few months the chief and his family joined Providence Missionary Baptist Church. He presented me with artwork for the walls of my study, and these artifacts kept me connected to Mother Africa. These visual objects were constant reminders of his mission and his goal of introducing Americans to the various countries in Africa and their cultures. Chief Adetunji wanted to debunk many of the assumptions and misconceptions about Africa. He wanted Americans to know that Africa is one of the most diverse continents in the world. When, for example, you go to Nigeria, you will find that there are 288 dialects spoken in this one country.

When the African Museum did not develop according to his expectations, he decided to close the downtown store and move to Kennesaw State University, about twenty miles north of Atlanta. He is now endeavoring to create an African rural village so that Americans can get a clearer insight into living conditions, relationships, art and values in Africa. Kennesaw State University is hosting the equivalent of an

African Chamber of Commerce. Inter-faith and inter-cultural aware-ness is essential for explaining the awesomeness of God.

When the Olympics came to Atlanta in 1996, many of the offi-cials were busy setting up venues for sales and other strategies to pay for the Olympics. Chief Tunde Adetunji was not interested in com-mercializing the Olympics; rather, he wanted to use the Olympics as a way of bringing people together. He thought it could be done through art and diverse forms of entertainment. He and I became kindred spir-its because we shared this bold idealism; we believed that everything could serve God's greater purposes of building the beloved commu-nity. When people become unafraid to cross barriers built by man, the world will be a better place.

I began this story by saying that one Sunday morning, a member, Chief Tunde Adetunji, met me after church and handed me a framed list of quotations and sayings from my sermons over the past sever-al years. When you establish honest, transparent relationships, your words seem to resonate with others.

Here are the quotes which Chief Tunde Adetunji felt blessed him, that I pray, in turn, will bless you.

Pastor Gerald Durley's prophetic utterances

First Corinthians 3:13 – 14 says we shall be rewarded for good works.

Godly exercise is the key to godly character.

You can't hide your influence.

A single light can provide hope in the darkest night.

To love to teach is one thing; to love those who teach is quite another.

*To take the fear out of living is to put your faith in the living God.
We plant the seed; only God gives the harvest.*

To forget the elderly is to ignore the wisdom of the years.

For a Christian, strength always comes after brokenness.
Don't let confidence replace your trust in God.

One truth from the Bible is worth more than all the wisdom of man.

We experience God's strengthening in the strain of our struggle.

The world rewards quick success; God rewards long-term faithfulness.

There would be no crown wearer in heaven had Christ not been the
cross bearer on earth.

Commitment to Christ goes hand-in-hand with commitment to
His church.

If God doesn't remove an obstacle, He will help us find a way around it.

No danger can come so near the Christian that God is not nearer.

A smile is a curve that can set things straight.

A true friend stays true to the end.

He is no genius who ignores his Creator.

The new measure of a person is what's in the heart.

Jesus doesn't need long years; he needs witnesses.

Those who lay up treasure in heaven are the richest people on earth.
When Jesus changes your heart, He gives you a heart for others.

The key to understanding the written word is knowing the living word.

At the heart of worship is worship from the heart.

God sometimes puts us in the dark to show us that Jesus is the light.

Our highest privilege is to talk to God; our highest duty is to listen to Him.

To face life's challenges, look at the unchanging God.

The best way to know God's will is to say, "Thy will be done."

The Bible – eternal truth and never fading nor failing beauty.

We don't really know the Bible until we obey the Bible.

Christians are either Bibles or libels.

In every desert of trial, God has an oasis of comfort.

Opportunities to be kind are never hard to find.

People will listen to you carefully if they see you living faithfully.

The question is not where God is but where he isn't.

If you are living for Christ, you may lose some friends but you won't lose their respect.

In a changing world, you can trust God's unchanging word.

True repentance turns from the wrong and returns to the right.

What is done for Christ in this life will be rewarded in the life to come.

Those who love God will love their neighbor.

It's always darkest just before the dawn.

Conscience is a trustworthy compass when God's word is your true North.

The right kind of fear will keep you from doing wrong.

There is no true happiness apart from holiness, and there is no holiness apart from Christ.

A gem cannot be polished without friction nor a man perfected without adversity.

Serving the Lord is an investment with eternal dividends.

These words were compiled by Chief Tunde Adetunji, African World Museum and Center, August 14, 2005

A Word from My Father

My father was a good man, but he struggled to tell us that he loved us. He felt that if he kept a roof over our heads, clothes on our backs, and food on the table, that his love was evident. I was in my thirties when I began to realize that Dad had been busy working, trying to take care of his children. That didn't occur to me as a young child when I felt alienated and unloved. The more I thought about it, though, the more I began to appreciate him. The godliness in him caused him to work hard, sacrifice and keep his family together and alive.

When my brother Dennis was killed in a traffic accident, my father and I were standing at the graveside when he turned to me and said, "I never really told Dennis that I loved him."

I said, "Daddy, you never told me that you loved me either."

"What do you mean, 'I never told you I love you'? Did you have a roof over your head, clothes on your back and food in your stomach?" To him, these actions were love. Wouldn't it be great to see more people acting in love?

I responded, "Yes, I had those things, but you never told me that you loved me."

On that day, standing by my brother's grave, nothing else was said.

Six months later I had an engagement in Milwaukee, where my

parents lived. Before I left, I told Muriel, "I'm going to sit down and talk with my father about why he never told me that he loved me." By this time, I was in my forties and when I confronted him, he said, "You know, Jerry, my father never told me that he loved me either."

I said to him, "Because your father never told you of his love is no reason for you to withhold expressing your love to me. Do you love me?"

Again, he said, "You know I love you. I have lived with your mother for fifty years, and we show our love by giving to each other."

Again I asked, "Do you love me?"

He repeated, "You know I love you."

"Yes, but I want to hear those words coming out of your mouth. You've shown me, you've been there for me, but you never said it to me!"

"Well, if you want me to, I'm willing to say it."

"I don't want you to say it because I want you to; I want you to say it because you feel it, because you feel love for me."

Finally, he said, "Jerry, I love you."

The hunger to hear the simple words "I love you" has become so important that I have begun to say to my children and my grandchildren, "I love you." For example, every time I talk to one of them on the telephone, I conclude before hanging up, "I love you." And I'm going keep on saying it because I need to say it and they need to hear it.

I realize that I lived a number of years without understanding my father's love, but in later years, we celebrated my twenty years of ministry at Providence Church together. Someone had the idea of writing my father and requesting him to send an affirmation to be read at our twentieth anniversary. Of course, it was a surprise to me, but when I read what he had written, I couldn't help remembering our conversation, first at the grave of my brother, and then in his home in Milwaukee. I think in this poetic offering, he is saying to the best of his ability that he loved me. I will never question the deep and sincere love my father showed me, and I quietly believe that I am who I am today because of my father and how he "showed" me love, not "told" me love.

FOR YOU, MY SON

Almost every day I'm touched
By something that reminds me of you

I'll come across an old photograph
Or a certificate you earned and received in school.

Today:
In the midst of your busy life,
May you have at least one moment to sit back and relax – –
When you don't have to do anything,
Or be anywhere but where you are at this moment.

This is a perfect time to remind you: how thrilled
I am because of you; and I wish you and your family
Such happiness, like that you have given
To me and many others that you have touched.

May you have a moment to reflect on the past years and
To look forward to all that may be waiting for you
In the years ahead.

But mostly, in that moment, may you realize here and
Now what to give your life to – – not just to you
But to everyone who knows you – – and
How wonderful it is to have you for my son.

May God continue to bless you in your ministry and
service for and with the Providence Baptist Church

Congratulations, Jerry, "This is your day!"

In Christian regard,
Dad

As I reflect on these three experiences, I am not only amazed, but I am overwhelmed by the power of words. Words bring light into darkness; words open up vast possibilities for hurting people; words usher in encouragement and hope. Words may never fully express our feelings and our struggles, but they do make a mark. I felt so grateful for the words spoken and written to me by my father, though I had to encourage him to share them. The kindness and openness of Chief Tunde Adetunji reassured me that people do listen to what is said in a sermon. And the woman whose name I have forgotten not only blessed me one Sunday morning, but she has blessed me with her witness by just telling me that she heard my feeble words. Sometimes we who preach God's Word grow weary; we wonder if our words make a difference and if the sacrifice is worth it. But then God sends people like these whom I have described to give encouragement and strength to make it through days of testing and doubt. Thanks be to God for His Word to us and for our words to one another! Tell some of the people in your life today just how important they are to you, and you too will be amazed at what you mean to them.

CHAPTER ELEVEN

✪

I Am Amazed at the Challenges Still Before Us

WHEN I THINK ABOUT THE PROBLEMS WE FACE in this world, in one sense I could say, "there is nothing new under the sun," but in another, I'd say the old issues keep coming back with new revealing insights. For example, the relationship between Blacks and whites has roots in the earliest days of America. These relationships came in one decade as segregation and in another, as problems with voter registration. Sexual issues have also been relevant from biblical days to yesterday's newspaper. We even find evidence of sexual impropriety in archaic writings. Society has established instructions with respect to marriage, homosexuality, and human trafficking – and now we are bombarded with related messages and patterns of behavior on social media. As I put my life into perspective, I recognize a variety of experiences that have conditioned my eyes to see, my ears to hear, and my heart to feel with respect to these issues. Like Mary, the mother of Jesus, I have pondered social justice in my soul; I have also pondered the sexual issues of marriage, gay rights and human trafficking. I have questioned the relevancy of climate change, energy efficiency and the vast political divide between Democrats and Republicans on these topics, which are so obvious in America today. With respect to each of these issues, I have undergone conditioning, both in my attitude and my response, which I will endeavor to express. I must say that I am a work in progress, subject to change as I am exposed to new and different data.

Issue: Prejudice

I am compelled to write about my feelings and concerns for equal justice for Blacks, Native Americans, Latinos and poor Americans, because these are complex issues facing us all. I was not always interested in these matters. Like many young African-Americans growing up in the 1940's-1960's, I had other pressing, survival-related concerns on my mind. Even though we lived in California, our house was in a segregated community. I didn't know it at the time because all we saw was that we were all poor. I went to school with whites, Latinos and Asians, but they were just as poor as my family. However, we kids really didn't see ourselves as poor. We went to separate churches but we played together, laughed together and did not realize that we were living in a racially and economically segregated section of Bakersfield. We survived in a poor Black community along with poor whites, Mexicans and Asians. I didn't know to call our situation segregated or unjust; it simply was the way life was for all of us. At the time, I had no idea what nationality some of the people were. I knew that they spoke other languages, were a different color, had a different hair texture, and worshipped their God in their own way.

Later, when I was thirteen or fourteen, I worked in the fields with seasonal immigrant workers, especially Mexicans, who had migrated across the river into California looking for any type of work. There appeared to me to be no discrimination when we were working together harvesting agricultural crops. When we left work under the hot California sun every day and boarded the bus to take us back into Bakersfield, I gradually began to notice that many of the Mexican families lived in shacks with five or six persons to a room. They came into California to earn money to send back to their families in Mexico, as many are doing today. I noticed the disparities even among those who were also poor. I didn't pay much attention to it because I was in a survival mode myself and was consumed with making as much money as I could.

After we moved to Denver and I attended Manual High School, I immediately sensed that there was a vast difference between those students who attended North, South, or East high schools. North, South and East were more upper-class; those in West High School were pre-dominately Mexican-American, poor and underprivileged. When schools played each other in basketball, there was always an undercurrent of racial tension. We ignorantly looked down on the students at West High. The feelings were mutual. Poor people need for there to be another group that's inferior to them too. West High was not too good in basketball because they concentrated on playing soccer. They were outstanding at soccer. In those days we made fun of the Mexicans – living in houses full of children, riding in a pickup truck with four abreast in the cab, eating tortillas and frijoles. Unfortunately, we stereotyped Mexicans just like whites stereotyped us. I was blind to the discrimination and felt no urge to try to change prevailing perceptions. I just accepted that this was the way life was and as long as it didn't hurt anyone, I was fine. Sound familiar?

I hate to admit now that I was totally oblivious to any concern about racial prejudice until I entered college and realized that I, too, was an object of racial and economic discrimination. Until this time, I had not realized the plight of African-Americans. After all, I lived in California and Colorado where discrimination was less overtly obvious. Arriving in Nashville, Tennessee, I quickly realized there was a great schism between me and the white citizens of Tennessee. Until I arrived in Nashville, I had never seen segregated drinking fountains or segregated restrooms. Everywhere I went in Nashville, I saw signs that said "White Only" over drinking fountains and in public waiting rooms. The South had a legalized and approved form of racism. Where I grew up, the racial attitudes were subliminal and covert, but in the South prejudice was well exposed and hidden from no one. At this point I realized that changes had to occur. Exposure is a great developer of character. Often people don't know who they really are until the veil of ignorance is lifted, allowing the "new" person to emerge.

When I heard Dr. King say, "None of us is free until all of us are free," I accepted the fact that we had a formidable task before us. This helped me to realize that if we sought to oppress the oppressors, we were no better than them. In my freshman and sophomore years, I began to think deeply about the injustice against African-Americans.

I had an emerging need to find ways that I could make a difference. From Nashville, I looked back toward Denver and realized that the Mexicans and Blacks there were simply trying to make it, trying to get an education, and trying to progress in life. I remembered how Blacks and Mexicans struggled against each other in Denver and Sacramento. I often thought, "We cannot fight with each other; we are minorities and we must not fight for crumbs among ourselves while the majority enjoys the fruits of our negative bickering."

Minorities like Blacks, Latinos and Jews must join together to give each other support in an insensitive racial climate like ours. Though I have said very little about my perspective and relationship with Jews, I recognize that their plight is similar to that of African-Americans. I grew up not understanding Jewish humor, religion or culture. Muriel was from New York and had attended school with Jewish people. So, she was able to explain to me what I needed to understand about Jewish culture. I had heard people say that the Jews control the media, that the Jews control the money, and so on and so forth. I had had the same feelings about Jewish people that I had about Latinos, until I faced blatant discrimination in my own life. These experiences taught me what prejudice and racism look and feel like. I quickly learned what it does to persons who are its object, how fear and ignorance feed prejudice and how we must come together to dispense with the alienating power of prejudice. These insights were implicit in my growing up among those who were different from me, but they did not become explicit until I arrived in Tennessee. God's chosen moments for growth and exposure are always impeccable.

Issue: Sexuality

My father's brother, my uncle Robert, was one of the closest family members I had. He was a homosexual, and my relationship with him shaped my attitude toward gays and lesbians, their relationship to each other and to the larger society. Early on I didn't know that he was homosexual, but I noticed that his behavior was different from other men. He never talked about his being gay; he was loving, he was understanding and he was a cherished friend to me.

After I had finished my freshman year at Tennessee State University, my uncle Robert asked me to come to Washington, D.C. and spend the summer with him. So I went to Washington. He found a job for me at his law firm. My horrible job was evicting people who did not pay their rent. I would go with the law firm employees to physically move the evicted resident's furniture from the house to the street. I noticed whenever we went anywhere, Robert always talked with all of the men. He laughed with them, touched them. He was really outgoing. On the weekend he invited friends over to the apartment for fellowship, and generally we went out together. At the time I did not understand homosexual behavior or recognize it. I was familiar with offensive words like sissy, homo and faggot, but I was naive about the true homosexual lifestyle. Though I was unfamiliar with the gay lifestyle, I knew that my uncle would never be inappropriate with me. He taught me to respect all people regardless of their color, economic status, physical appearance, or sexual orientation.

With respect to gay and lesbian people, Robert taught me a number of good lessons. He'd say, "Today's business is tomorrow's competition," by which he meant competition for intimate relationships among people of the same gender. This could apply to many situations, but he explained to me that a gay man or gay woman often endeavors to reach out to a new person to initiate a relationship. I never heard Robert say a negative word about anyone, and he taught me that vital lesson for life.

One day he introduced me to his friend Walter Jones. Today, I suppose that we would say Walter was his partner, or lover. Walter and I were the same age, eighteen years old. When we were not working, Robert would ask Walter to take me out and show me the city. Over time, Walter and I became good friends. Robert had always cautioned me never to judge people, never to blame them for something they could not help. I had discussions with Robert about whether gay people were born homosexual or whether their environment pushed them in that direction. As we talked about it, I would say things like, "God created Adam and Eve, not Adam and Steve." And Robert would always caution me, "Never speak down to a person, but respect all persons for who they are." I experienced a new level of awareness from these talks with my uncle. Often when we went out, Robert would say to me, "Look at that guy over there! Or, look at that sweet thing standing over there." I looked and all I saw was a 245-pound man; my reaction was vastly different from Robert's. Sometimes he'd walk up to a big, muscular man and say, "Hello, Sweetie." The man would wink at him and smile like he got the message. During this time, very few gay people came out of the closet, but in social situations they had gestures, movements and codes that enabled them to make contact with each other. I realized that the more you genuinely seek to know people and their circumstances, the greater your level of appreciation and respect for them. People are different and we must appreciate their differences, even though we might not fully comprehend them.

While I've never been one to judge anyone because of his or her sexuality, I do believe that many in the gay and lesbian community suffer a great deal of pain and hurt. I believe that they face substantial psychological repression from the outside world and, therefore, remain in the closet, trying to be something that they are not. As a psychologist, I have urged a number of people to accept and embrace who they truly are. I have often been asked, "Did God create me this way?" I usually respond by saying, "I'm not God. Only God is God and knows the answer to that question."

I urge people to be who they are today. Three weeks from now, they may be different. It is important to me for them to know that I am commanded to love them right now, for whoever they are. Under the power of acceptance we gain a clearer understanding of each other; only then can we move forward together.

There is goodness in all people. We need to learn to see the good in others. To become the person God has ordained you to be requires the ability to be open to those who may be completely different or opposed to your way of life. Therefore, it is essential to communicate for understanding, rapport, and trust if we are to live as God ordained us. I believe that homosexual people can experience love that is as strong and deep as a man and woman can. I have pondered this for a number of years, and I remain open for growth and understanding.

Issue: Pornography

Other sexual issues faced in today's world are pornography, prostitution and sex trafficking. I did not realize the pervasiveness of pornography until seven or eight years ago, when a man confessed his addiction to pornography to me. After this first confession I discovered that a number of men, especially white men, are captured by this addiction. Through these experiences, I became profoundly conscious of the number of pornography shops and sex stores in the city. When men become enslaved to pornography, it affects their work life, their relationships with friends, and their families. Sexual addiction especially impacts children in many adverse ways.

To respond to the pervasive presence of pornography, a group of concerned lay people and pastors formed an organization to study the influence of pornography and ways to curb it in our community. Very soon we found out that pornography is a progressive addiction. A man who begins with pornographic books soon progresses to videos; from videos he may expand his taste from tame to violent sex; the next stage explores experimental sex with multiple partners, and so on. I learned that some men and women are even exploring bestiality. Once the addiction has fully captured a person, the appetite becomes increasingly demanding. Due to its sometimes violent nature, sex addiction must be curbed early on. Before we began studying the problem, I had no idea there were 410 sex shops in Atlanta, Georgia alone.

As if we were being challenged, a sex shop opened in our area of ministry. We went to the manager and informed him that we intended to take pictures of everyone who went in and came out of his place of business. We explained to him that we would post the photos outside on the street for everyone to see. To give him an out, a member of the City Council and I asked him to close the shop, but he would not. I invited a dozen preachers to stand with me on the sidewalk across the street and to observe all who went in and out. This sex shop was opened just a few yards from an Islamic mosque; its location was illegal and this violation of the law was one of the factors that enabled us to close it quickly.

One night, several of my friends and I went into the shop and the owner said, "You've been standing on the street, taking pictures, blowing horns and flashing lights trying to alienate my customers. Every Sunday you preachers give people what you think they need. You tell them what is lacking in their lives, and then you try to sell them your answer. I give people what they want. I don't have to do any persuading. All my customers are eager; I have only to open the door and let them in. You preachers could probably benefit from what I have to offer."

I responded, "You may give them what they want, and I may give them what I think they need, but I tell you this. You are going to get living hell from me and my partners until you close this shop down. I don't know whether you want it or you need it, but you're surely going to get it." Eventually, the man moved his sex shop from our community.

Issue: Prostitution and Trafficking

Atlanta recently began to have difficulty with young girls engaging in sex for money. I became acquainted with Dr. Scott Weimer, a member of our group who was also the pastor of the North Avenue Presbyterian Church, and he explained to me how Christian laypeople work with girls on the street. They speak with them and counsel with them about getting out of prostitution. An organization here in Atlanta, "Street Grace," has, as its singular mission, rescuing young girls and women from lives of prostitution. Many of the girls are runaways, stowaways and the like, who were actually kidnapped and brought to this country to be hired out for sex.

Our intention to rid our city of this lurid side of life led us to the Gold Club. The Gold Club was a gentlemen's gathering place to have drinks, observe nude dancing and spend time in private rooms with available women who would respond to a man's bidding. After I learned what was happening in this club, I was furious and highly motivated for change. Since I don't know how to do anything halfway, I set my mind to close the Gold Club. I spoke to a pastor friend of mine and invited him to join me in the mission to close the Gold Club. His response was, "No. I can't do that; I don't feel that God called me to shut down the Gold Club." I wondered what he felt he was called by God to do.

It is incumbent upon all of us who have any degree of a moral compass, to join forces to challenge those who would enslave our young women into a life of trafficking and prostitution. This darkness exists all over the world, but we can do something to change it if we are willing to stand up and sacrifice our positions for those who have been allocated to the fringes of society. I am amazed at how quiet and unconcerned we become when we are not personally affected by an issue. Human deprivations and senseless insensitivity to the sanctity of human life have encouraged me to dedicate the rest of my life to uplifting those who have grown weary of fighting the daily battle of survival.

Issue: Climate Change

Climate change used to be one of the furthest thoughts from my mind. But then, a friend invited me downtown to view a movie called "The Great Warming." Initially, it did not impress me at all. What did I care about toxins in the air? What did polluted water and an excess of carbon dioxide have to do with my life? I was incensed that I had wasted my time, but being a nice guy, I endured the movie. The person showing the film was present that day in the theater. At the conclusion of the movie she said, "I believe we have a pastor here in the house" – and she asked me to pray. Before I prayed, she said, "We need to convince people of the crisis we are facing. I'm not a religious person, but I do believe that the faith community can enlighten the public because you speak every week to a large base of people who trust you."

Then she said to me, "I don't know how you responded to the film tonight, but would you pray for awareness of the climate change movement? Pray that what we are doing will manifest itself and get attention in the coming years because we are destroying God's earth." Something moved me and I began to pray right there in the theater. My hostess for the evening said, "I knew that we had brought the right person to see this film." There are times when God is orchestrating every thought, action and reaction in your life.

I said, "What right person?"

She said, "The right person to get a movement started because we must make a difference and save the planet."

After this conversation at the theater, we went next door and sat down in a restaurant to have a bite to eat. No sooner had we sat down than she me, "How did you get people committed to the Civil Rights Movement?"

I tried to answer. "First of all, we had a cause, a moral issue." But, as we began to talk, I realized that global warming, drastic climate change, energy inefficiency and the greenhouse gas effect were all moral causes. And it hit me clearly, "To destroy creation is immoral." As we continued talking, I realized that the concerns we were discussing were already negatively affecting the people that I served. Establishing toxic waste dumps and transporting toxic materials with their dangerous side effects through our communities affected the lives of human beings on a daily basis. I began to comprehend that in states where strip-mining prevails and trees are bulldozed, that there's nothing left to take the carbon dioxide from the air, and replenish the oxygen. These issues began to mushroom in my brain and bring conviction to my heart. I was compelled to seek ways to get more involved with impacting the perils of not challenging climate change.

From that encounter after the movie, I was asked to go to New Mexico to the National Environmental Fund Raisers Association. Those who sent me said, "Just speak from your heart." So I went, and the group sat around talking about what they were planning to fund, which grant writer they would use to raise the money, etc., and I judged these as some of the dullest conversations I'd ever heard in my life. They were powerful, well-educated and committed people, but they were not enthusiastic. After sitting for several days, they said to me, "Dr. Durley, we would like for you to respond to what you have heard. Maybe we can learn from what you did in the Civil Rights Movement."

I began, "You folks don't have a movement. You're talking to each other, but nobody knows what you're talking about. What you do sounds good and looks good, but you need to speak with passion! Enthusiasm with facts and conviction will inspire people to act. We have to have enthusiasm and we must be understood.

"Every week we preachers talk about things you cannot see. For example, we mention heaven every week and you can't see it. Nobody knows where heaven is; I guess it's up, but I don't know. We sell pearly gates and streets of gold, but nobody knows what they are. We speak of holy garments, but I sure don't want to wear a white robe. Pearly gates are ugly and streets of gold would be too soft to be durable. Yet, we convincingly tell people that that is what they want and need. That's the power of the faith community.

"In the faith community, we present a vision that makes the difference between life and death; your movement was also born in response to a life and death issue. However, the environmental movement is not speaking with a sense of urgency. You say, 'Well, next month we are visiting this toxic waste dump . . .' but there is no enthusiasm! Excitement is contagious; dullness deadens! You remind me of a group of people who have just gotten out of the grave and are getting ready to go back in it. If you are not excited about your vision, who else will be? No one can start a movement without that kind of energy. My advice is, if you can't create that kind of excitement, get someone to help you who can.

"You asked me to help you. I can't do that. I am busy getting kids out of jail, putting food on the table for the elderly, working to repair broken marriages and trying to look after my own family. Last week a woman in Georgia showed a film and asked me to pray for her efforts, and here I am in New Mexico speaking to the National Environmental Fund Raisers Association. I am enthusiastic about what you are doing, and I advise you to get excited and enthusiastic about your cause. When you do, positive energy will be created, followed by sustainable results."

Issue: Renewable Energy

An urgent issue that we must face in the twenty-first century is the discovery and creation of renewable energy. It's become an issue that I've expressed concern about many times. During a conversation with government officials regarding energy, the comment was made that they thought I was mainly involved in civil and human rights. I replied, "I am interested in civil and human rights, but I can't do anything about those issues if I'm dead from a toxic environment." Revelations like these force us to engage with all the problems surrounding renewable energy. It requires that we educate ourselves on our options. I have to learn about things like 'fracking,' which is a new drilling technology that makes it possible to reach natural gas when it's seemingly out of reach. I have to understand 'shale', which is a fine-grained, sedimentary rock composed of mud that is a mix of flakes of clay minerals and tiny fragments of other minerals that can be refined for fuel. And, I have to understand the various uses of natural gas. There are so many unforeseeables around energy that are vital to the health of this country, and we cannot fail to be vigilant on this issue.

Today, two of the most prevalent issues are global warming and climate change. To educate myself, I traveled to England and familiarized myself with all the uses of wind to produce energy. I went to Germany, where they have less sunlight than we do in Georgia, but they are creating solar panels and harnessing the energy of the sun. America uses more limited amounts of solar energy because our energy companies have not figured out how to calculate it and still balance their bottom lines. They make more money when they generate energy from coal or gas or nuclear power. In ten or fifteen years, the U.S. will be a nuclear country because nuclear energy offers one of the cleanest and least expensive ways to create energy. One of the reasons we haven't gone completely nuclear today is because companies are still researching how to safely eliminate the waste. It is also very expensive to build a nuclear plant; it requires years of construction and a great deal of water for a nuclear installation. Once these obstacles are overcome, America will be a nuclear country.

Issue: Poverty and Violence

President Lyndon Johnson began what we call "the war on poverty". Poverty is the war that we are losing. The gap between the rich and the poor continuously grows wider and wider. It is not a matter of economics; but rather, how does America make the "American Dream" equally accessible to all?

Once again, we must begin to actively engage in the war on violence. The phrase alone is such an oxymoron: 'War' on 'Violence.' Violence is everywhere and not just violence alone, but the mental illness that lies beneath so much of the violence. The news reported in 2013 that a soldier suffering from Post-traumatic Stress Disorder (PTSD) killed Chris Kyle, a 38-year-old Navy SEAL who was the number one military sniper in the world. Where did this happen? Not at a school, or a shopping center, or a church. But on a firing range! The solider suffering from PTSD walked up to the sniper on a firing range and shot his hero in the head. Violence is not because of poverty as some say; we know this because the poorest countries in the world have less violence than we do. We must attack the attitude and environment which creates a violent society and put effective services in place for those individuals who need assistance.

Issue: A Divided Country

Today, America is being led by fear and ignorance. We all get in our little boxes and threaten the people on the outside, and every threat increases fear. There seems to be a striking contradiction. Even though we have access to more knowledge than we've ever had, our ignorance is causing us to engage in practices that are totally idiotic. Because America is being fueled by absolute fear, we are divided. We are in more segregated groups now than ever before. The Jews are here. The Muslims are there. The Whites are here. The Blacks and the Liberals are over there. The Conservatives are over here; and we are all clinging to our comfort zones. How is it that we are uncomfortable in our comfort zone? We must learn to break down the barriers, expand our comfort zones, and join hands together; in this friendship circle we will create a wall that can resist any division. However, if a person is not prepared to leave his or her comfort zone, I contend that we need to help them stretch the boundaries of their comfort zone. Fortunately for us, the young people are beginning to break down the barriers with their fresh perspective, access to social media and their ever-expanding technological social networks.

As the Bible says of Esther, "You have come to the kingdom for such a time as this." Perhaps this is a fitting label for Barack Obama, who seems to be the right man for this hour. He was born in Hawaii of a white mother and a Black father; he was reared in Indonesia by his mother and later in Hawaii by his maternal grandparents. He was educated in law at Harvard University, but he worked on the streets of Chicago organizing and educating for justice. He served in the Illinois State Senate from 1997-2004, when he was elected to the U. S. Senate. He then was elected twice to be the President of the United States. As the president, he has dealt with many controversial matters: poverty, violence, prejudice, immigration, women's issues, human sexuality, abortion rights, gun control, climate warming, equal education insurance coverage for all, and raising up a strong middle class. He has made a difference!

I am glad that I lived to see this day. We have an opportunity to build a great nation if we can come together with an open mind and an open heart to seek a middle ground that includes all Americans. I have worked for this new day, and I will continue to work in my own way to make a difference in the world. The challenges which we have and will face will be positively overcome when we as a people recognize, understand, respect, and trust one another. We have more in common than what is dividing us. Each of us must vow to make a difference by overcoming our ignorance and fears. I am there now, and I AM AMAZED!!

CHAPTER TWELVE

✪

I Am Amazed at the Demand for New Life

HAVE YOU EVER WITNESSED A RESURRECTION? I mean have you ever seen someone rise from the dead? This actually happens to people in the world today. I am interested in these people. I'm interested in seeing people come alive. I am interested in people, helping people come alive to their situation and opportunity. What is the value of struggling with the oppressive issues in our society, if nothing happens in the hearts of individuals? If you reduce the situation of individuals to a common denominator, one thing matters most – a person being alive physically, psychologically and spiritually, feeling good about oneself. A nation wants to feel good about itself, a state wants to feel good about itself, a community wants to feel good about itself, and it is individual people, people who feel good about themselves, that drive these corporate institutions.

Those seeking to live in the rhythm of their lives may be poor people, successful business people or they could be a family or a community organization. I would like to engage these different facets of society and help every individual and every group to achieve a feeling of confidence and hope. When that change comes, it makes a major difference in a life. When it makes a difference in one life, it makes a difference in the home and when it makes a difference in the home, it makes a major difference in the community. When the community is transformed, it will give birth to a new order.

Every person must first deal with his or her own challenges. How can you help someone else when you have not helped yourself? You have to be free yourself if you hope to free others. What may be truth for you today may be false tomorrow. Since truth is ever evolving, we must be open to the truth of this day and this hour. Relative to this point in my life, my wife plays an extremely significant role. She is always asking me the right questions: Do you really believe that? Is this what you really need to do? Every day she helps me search for and find my own truth, though she seldom makes speeches or outwardly embraces every cause. She is so gifted at encouraging me to face my shortcomings and futuristic ideas. She amazes me.

Moments of Aliveness

When I think of aliveness in my life, I recall those basic formative experiences; recalling them today puts me in contact with the source of my passion to see other people come alive.

When my grandmother sent us children out to play in the rain and the mud puddles, I felt alive, truly as alive as a six-year old could feel. When she cut newspaper and put it in my shoe to cover a hole and told me to hold up my head and smile, I felt alive.

When I was ten years old and in the fourth grade and a stuttering teacher invited me to speak to her class and I didn't stutter, I felt alive.

When Mr. Martin made a bust of me from plaster of Paris, as he handed it to me with these words, "You can be tough like this bust," he helped me to feel alive.

When John B. McLendon visited me in Denver and invited me to attend Tennessee State University, something in me came alive and I began to imagine myself as a star basketball player. When you feel alive, you can believe in your dreams and they will come true.

When I was in the Peace Corps and taught those young men in Nigeria new ways of farming, I was fulfilled and exuded joy in life. When I met Muriel West in Neuchatel, Switzerland, the centerpiece of my heart slipped into place and I felt alive.

When I entered Northern Illinois University, I was given respect, entrusted with important decisions and learned the finer skills of leadership, which gave me a feeling of aliveness and a great sense of fulfillment.

199

When I was in Washington, D.C. working with highly respected men and women on issues that concerned Black colleges and universities, I felt alive knowing that I was creating something that could change Black people's world.

When the nurse said to me, "Your son is alive," I felt a mixture of joy and gratitude which sprang from the core of my soul—ALIVENESS!!

When I moved to Atlanta and began work at Clark College and Morehouse School of Medicine, my daily assignments brought me in touch with young Black men and women who were seeking their way in life, and I had the joy of walking with them through their present and into their future.

When I reached out to the poor and broken and when I challenged the laws that oppressed them, I felt that I had been created for such a task.

All these facets of my experience illustrate, in part, what I mean by coming ALIVE NOW. Though no single memory captures all of what it means to come alive, if we put them together, we would have a mosaic of what it truly means!

Come Alive Again

As I have reflected on the issues facing us, I believe that at the core of the problem is the need to come alive. So, I will spend the next years of my life enabling people to Come Alive Again: **A.L.I.V.E. – – "A Life Is Valuable Everyday."**

I can envision this theme in my mind today: You drive up behind a car and you see a bumper sticker that says, "A Life Is Valuable Every Day. Come alive again!" People need to come alive again! Our schools need to come alive again! Our churches need to come alive again! Our legislatures need to come alive again! Our homes need to come alive again! I need to come alive again! Some of us, because of circumstances beyond our control, have died inside. We have given up and are emotionally and spiritually DEAD!

To come alive again signifies that we were once alive, but something changed and now we are not. We have gone to sleep. There's something in each of us that needs to come back alive. Your children may be on drugs or your friend may be in jail, your grandmother may be sick or your marriage difficult – all of these persons can come alive again! Helping people come alive again really excites me; it will consume the rest of my life. I don't know how to get there, but I have a vision of a whole person in a whole society, and I want others to see and strive with me to create that society. In my waking hours, this consumes my thoughts; it crowds my dreams when I am asleep at night. Can you envision a family, community, church or world where people are truly alive to the vast possibilities of living in peace, joy and love?

The Miracle of Birth and Rebirth

There's something marvelous and miraculous about being alive. When we were born, the doctor gave us a pat on the bottom and we came alive and shouted. We began to grow and develop and then engage the physical world by crawling, walking, and running. These three activities symbolically follow us throughout life: we begin new activities, like work, by crawling; we rise up to walk to the next level, then we run until we can't run anymore. And then we die. When we die, we realize that if there is not a miracle of resurrection, we will be no more. We're dead. *We cannot come alive again without the help of God.*

Not only is there a physical birth, but there is also a spiritual birth, a rebirth of a sort. A yearning in us cries out, "I long to know more than physical life; I can, I will, I must, because the God who created the world and all of us wanted something more from our days here on earth." The spiritual life in us overflows into the lives of our friends, our neighbors, our close associates and when we are giving ourselves to this life, we are truly alive ourselves. Life produces life! We are alive in our churches. We are alive in our marriages. We are alive on our jobs. Everything around us may be gloomy, but we are alive because we have that spark within us that becomes the light that guides us. Living this life gives us a sense of meaning and purpose in everything we do.

Challenges to Aliveness

But this aliveness is not without its challenges. Early on, the struggles of this journey begin to invade us: divorce, death, misunderstandings, and illnesses, to name a few. All of these negative forces are a challenge to life and its fulfillment. The battle gets old and the people get weary. The interplay of three forces drives us toward these challenges – frustration, anger and bitterness. First comes frustration. When we are frustrated, we don't know which way to turn; we sometimes feel we cannot even move. Following on the heels of frustration comes anger, the inner rage about situations that we cannot change. Anger retained and stuffed down becomes bitterness, and with bitterness all of life takes on a dark shade of gray. After bitterness has ground away at us for weeks, months or years, it finally destroys the vitals at the core of our being. When we reach this point, our situation seems hopeless, we see no way to respond to our challenges, and a worse plight awaits us – the pit of depression.

Unless we do something with our depression, we will find it harder and harder to get up in the morning. At this point our souls are spiritually dead. Life has no meaning, no joy, no sense of direction, and unhappiness corrupts our days.

I turned on the television one night and caught part of a disturbing show called "The Walking Dead." The name aptly describes the person who has fallen into the pit of depression and can find no way out. Such unfortunate souls are not living; they are merely existing.

A good friend of mine of over twenty years has sometimes seemed like the walking dead. I first met him when he was eighteen years old and entering college. At the time, I was the Dean at Clark College. After he finished college and was climbing the corporate ladder, his wife developed a brain tumor. As they were getting ready to go to a football game between the Saints and the Falcons, she developed a terrible headache which caused him to put her in the hospital. She entered the hospital on a Thursday; the next day she went into a coma and was moved from DeKalb Medical Center to Grady Hospital. On Monday she died.

At her death she left a twelve-year-old daughter and her spouse.

Her husband, a banker and investment man, plunged into a deep, deep depression. I tried to talk to him then and again a few weeks later. I spoke with him, but the challenges were apparent.

In his confusion and grief, he said to me, "Pastor, there's nothing left in me; I take my daughter to a dance lesson or to practice a game, I take her to a movie, but my wife is gone." Shock, frustration, anger and grief had engulfed his life; he was in the pit. I had to stand by and let him find his way; at this stage of grief it was difficult for him to reach out for, or receive, help. He is among the walking dead. He has not found a way to come alive again. He's dead now, but he can come alive again. I sincerely hope that he can find something that really excites him and enlivens his spirit. He can find his passion once again. He has to get his previous passion back; it's there, it's really there, but it has to be uncovered and liberated so that he can look at his life and realize that 'A Life is Valuable Everyday' – he can be ALIVE!

The experience I have described is not limited to this man; all of us meet people who are struggling for meaning in their lives. When we talk with people who are suffering in the pit, we realize that they are dead internally. They may be going through the motions of life, but they manifest a spirit of death. Everywhere young men and women are facing struggles with meaninglessness, and they want to come alive. They have had everything the world offers – cars, clothes, a good education, decent paying jobs, and though they have these things, something is missing in their lives. Unless they find their way they will die; even now they are among the seriously ill. With life all around them, they are in the intensive care unit of life. Walking the pathway packed by the footsteps of the crowd is not bringing life.

Many of these young people are looking toward the older generation to give them the answer, to guide them through uncharted waters. They're waiting for us to pass on to them the ways of life, but many of us don't have anything to offer them because we are also dead – our flame has become a flicker. I realize that we cannot do anything about our physical death, but we can do something about our mental, emotional, psychological and spiritual death. We can come alive again!

How do we come alive? What does it mean to come alive? It means to find within ourselves that spark, that emotional surge that inspires us every morning to get out of bed and take on the challenges of the day. The acronym "A.L.I.V.E." – **A** **L**ife **I**s **V**aluable **E**veryday – offers a foundational statement. Every single day, every hour of the day, each of us has value, and we choose how to respond to the happenings of the day. Our lives are not defined by what we have been, whom we have known, what we've attained or what we possess! If you find yourself on the wrong path, you might consider making some different and difficult decisions. If we do not have something worth living for, we need to uncover what would satisfy our lives. You can find that spark within; look into your deep memory, find that life which was once meaningful, ignite that spark again and come alive. Look upward first for guidance then inward for direction.

Coming alive becomes an urgent issue when you recognize that everything you do is meaningless and dull; it no longer has the spark. You live with a nonchalant attitude – if I do it, it's okay; if I don't do it, it's okay. You're suffering death because you don't have anything that gives excitement or meaning to your life.

I know that I have been blessed more than many people: I have my health, I have my strength and I have a good family. So I want to look up and journey on, until I become the person that I was created to be. Life is a cycle of continuous experiences. Each experience should contribute to a raison d'être. You are here for a reason, for a purpose.

If you think that your way is tough, compare it with this gut-wrenching story. One of my assistants at the church, Ken, who was also a high-grade employee at Emory Hospital, was an amazing man. After he retired from the military, he and his wife, Cindy, moved to Atlanta. A short time later, they were having lunch at their kitchen table when Cindy suddenly put down her sandwich and said, "I don't feel well." They left immediately to get her checked out. By the time they got to the hospital, she was drifting into a coma. Ken asked the doctors what was going on and they said, "We don't know."

He responded, "Well, let me go home and pick up a few things that she will need for a stay in the hospital." Before he could get home, the hospital called him back. The person on the phone said, "You'd better come back. We don't know what is happening to your wife, but it is serious." He returned at once.

You need to understand the current of energy that flowed through this man; he was always the life of the party. He had been a colonel in the military and was accustomed to being the center of attention. He had a light and easy spirit wherever he went.

He called me from the hospital that day and described what was happening. When I got to the hospital, he said, "She seems to be brain-dead." I tried to encourage him by reminding him that every doctor in the Emory system was available to him, and that the Emory doctors would do whatever was needed to assist his wife.

He said, "She can't die. She just can't. I retired from military service and our children are going to college. Now and for all time my dreams are being wiped out. She is only forty-nine years old. What is this?" God's timing unfortunately does not coincide with our wants, wishes, and desires.

The doctor indicated that we could take out the tubes when Ken consented. The doctor said, "If she can breathe on her own for fifteen minutes, we will continue to keep her on life support." We prayed about the decision to disconnect from the life support system. They proceeded to disconnect the tubes. Her breath came out and a deep yawn gave an outward sign of life. My friend and I jumped for joy. But, she immediately dropped back into a stupor. Her activity when the tubes were taken out was a natural reaction to the oxygen that had built up in her system. In a sense, her husband also died at the very moment she did. He fell to the floor and began pounding the tile and crying out, "How can I make it? How can I go on?"

The hospital had apartments across the street for the families of patients. We escorted him to one of the apartments and he fell into a deep sleep; he was dead with grief. When I came by to visit with him, the shades were always pulled down. In our conversation, one day he said, "I better go by the house and get a few things." From the time they had left until that moment, he had not been back to his house. I drove him home. We got out and entered the house. On the table was the piece of sandwich that Cindy had been eating when they jumped up and drove to the hospital.

After a number of months, Ken was still despondent and emotionally paralyzed. Every day he struggled to get out of bed; he had no hope or expectation for his future. One day I said to him, "Ken, God has not forsaken you. There is hope for the future; you can trust in the promises of Christ." All my words were to no avail. He could not even hear me; there was no life-giving power for him in what I was saying. I said to him, "It's been nine months since she passed, and it's now time for you to come back from the edge of the pit."

He said, "Gerald, I have nothing to live for." I responded, "You've got two children and a grandchild, and Cindy did a great job raising them. They need you."

Still grieving, he said, "I was always working and she had all the family responsibilities dumped on her."

He was blaming himself, living off his self-pity because he was emotionally and spiritually dead.

I argued with him, "You are fifty-one now, and you have a life ahead of you; come alive and leave your deadness."

After I had verbally struggled with him for more than an hour, we went down to a beer garden in Atlanta. At this particular bar, they had German beer and hand-rolled cigars. He had been in the military in Germany and had seen those big cigars before. The bar also served Wiener schnitzel, which I'd never had. We ordered beer and Wiener schnitzel and he began to talk about Cindy and how they had eaten Wiener schnitzel in Germany. Suddenly, Ken began to laugh, and it was the first time I had heard him laugh for more than a year.

He looked over at me and said, "Let me light your cigar."

He continued, "I remember how Cindy and I used to go to places like this in Germany and share a beer, and I just remembered how much fun it was."

I kept the conversation going. "If you like doing this, why can't we do it more often? Maybe we can do more of this and invite Muriel or your children? This is the beginning of the rest of your life.

"I urge you, Ken, to go back and teach your Bible class because you are a good teacher and you have not taught for some time. You were once so alive."

Ken was on his way to coming alive again!

Taking Ken's experience as an example, we see that many of the crises of life are unpredictable and senseless. It is the chaotic aspect of these events that tends to shake our world. Note that Ken had his life neatly laid out – he served his time in the military, retired and got a highly respectable position. When his wife died suddenly, it was like a bomb exploding under his dream, which blew the dream to smithereens. The impact was so drastic that he could not get hold of himself for more than a year. As in so many instances, when he was ready, he set aside his grief and a miracle happened.

Other Aspects of the Healing Process

By calling this healing, I am referring to the renewal of hope, the recovery of a vision and the realization of a dream. The first step in coming alive is to recognize: I am dead. Inside my gut I have reached the limits of my human capabilities; there's nothing that I can do to heal myself. But I need something or someone to make me whole. Will I find it in another person? Will I find it in a product? Will I find it in a position? Will I find it in a set of principles? Where will I find the energy that sparks my life? Perhaps it is a prize that is readily available: "This is the day that the Lord has made; I will rejoice and be glad in it." (Psalm 118:24) On the day that I claim it as God's gift, I get out of bed, open the blinds and even though it may be raining, I feel joyful and glad because I have a day God has created for me. My confidence in a sovereign God is the source of my joy.

I want to help people look daily into the mirror and realize that though life has become challenging, they can say to the image in the mirror, "I'm doing fine." Even though my life may seem miserable and circumstances are against me, there is still a reason for me to live. Look again into that mirror and say to yourself, "I am not dead because God is not finished with me yet." You may not know how to respond to this emptiness, but trust that there is a fullness awaiting you. We do not view persons' lives by where they have come from; we do not look at what happened in the past; we look at now, at what they are doing now, which is the most important point of view. I should not pray that God will change my circumstances, but that God will change me. To come alive, we must have God's divine remedy for change. I can ask God to change me and also to help me change me. When I am transformed, I can adapt to circumstances which are killing me daily by facing the losses and challenges of the present moment.

In so many ways, the death knell sounds over families, churches and communities. The smell of death is not only in us, but it is also in the institutions of our culture. So, we are becoming a world of human beings to whom nothing makes sense. When I read in the newspaper about a fourteen-year-old boy shooting a one-year-old baby in the face, or when I find that two young men have bombed the Boston Marathon, or when I listen to the story of a demented mind who went into Sandy Hook Elementary School and killed twenty-six children and adults, I see pictures of the meaninglessness I am describing. Daily newspapers are filled with stories that illustrate this point. There's a saying, "Hurting people hurt people." I believe that dead people kill people. Death is not only the plight of individuals. It's the plight of the environment on this planet. Greed and the demand for more are forcing us to rape the planet to sustain our vain lifestyles. All of these forces are coming together in one enormous thrust, seeking to destroy goodness, meaning, purpose and hope. But all of these negative signs and forces of deadness cannot keep us from coming alive again – A Life Is Valuable Everyday.

I believe that for people to come alive again, they must accept the fact that they are not in charge. We are not in charge of anything but the power to choose our pathway. We are not in charge of our life, nor are we in charge of our death. We are in charge only of what we do with what we have been given. God has given us a passion, and that passion knows what we are and what we need to do. If we can but uncover the surging power in the depths of our being, life will be different. When we lose our passion, we are dead; when our passion gets lost under other commitments, we soon die. It is the rediscovery of that passion that helps us come alive. Is there anything we are doing, that we would continue doing, whether we get paid or not?

I must emphasize that when the passion is gone, we are dead. When the passion of this nation's leaders is gone, when the passion of our churches is gone, when the passion of our children is gone, what do we have left? When the passion of honestly governing people is dead, we get the kind of government we have today. So the question that we must continually ask ourselves is, "What is the passion of my life?" What is it that I feel that I must do on this earth? What are the things I really desire to do? When we begin to get in touch with our true passion, it inspires other energy in our being, and we are then prepared to make the sacrifice for whatever it takes to achieve our goal.

Everything around us is energy, walking or talking, hard-driving or dancing – it's all energy. How do we take the energy that has been arrested and suppressed within us and turn it loose again? Obviously, this energy must be directed, because like water when it is not directed, it becomes a destructive flood. When we direct water, we call it irrigation. What do we call passion under control? Creativity! We want to take this water of life and use it to irrigate our passion, so that our passion will grow and propel our lives forward.

The lust for more money often quenches our true passion, a truth particularly applicable to young people. These young lives are the soil in which good seed are planted and grow into something great for the future. Jesus taught us about the soil. If the seeds fall on the path, the birds eat them up; if the seeds fall on stony ground, they take root quickly, spring up, but soon perish; and if the seeds fall among weeds, the weeds spring up and choke them; but if the seeds fall on good ground, they will multiply and bring forth an abundant harvest. The meaning is deceitfully simple – good seeds in good ground produces an abundant harvest. But, as they grow, they must be nurtured!

I talk to young people who frequently say, "I'm tired of this rat race, I'm tired of working day and night; I'm working harder and getting less."

I tell them, "I'm not getting in the rat race until I see a rat that's won it. I'll try to keep up with the Jones's when I find out who the Jones's are." Our young people must have the tools that will help them recognize when mental and spiritual death are setting in. They need insight into themselves so that they will not develop the symptoms of sickness that lead to death. We must devote our attention to helping them.

I spent nine years at the Morehouse School of Medicine, and I learned that America operates on the medical model, rather than the prevention model – fixing what is broken, rather than preventing the break. We get symptoms of headaches and fevers. We go to the doctor to get it fixed, but what if we had paid more attention to what we ate, the rest we got or the exercise we practiced? Would this prevent the headache? We must become more attentive and sensitive to ourselves and those around us who are in the intensive care of emotional and spiritual death. We must be proactive, and not reactive.

Recalling a day at Morehouse College brings to mind an experience that I recently had when I went by the college to pick up two tickets to the graduation ceremony that was to be conducted in a couple of days. It was a busy day. I was extremely busy during the early morning and just before noon I went by the college to pick up my tickets. As I was approaching the office where I was to get the tickets, I heard a voice calling out, "Dr. Durley, Dr. Durley!" and I turned to see a young man in his gown, holding his graduation hat in his hand, and running toward me. I stopped and waited.

When he got close he said, "You probably don't recall my name. I'm Steven Harris, and I came here four years ago to attend Morehouse College. The college was somewhat reluctant to admit me, but with my persistence, they finally did. It has been four years and in two days I will be walking across that platform getting my degree. And, do you know that I would never have made it, if it had not been for you."

When I heard those words, I was awestruck. What had I done? What did he mean that he would not have gotten the degree, if it had not been for me? I asked him, "What do you mean, Steven? How am I responsible for your getting this degree?"

With a big smile on his face, he said, "You probably don't remember it, but you addressed the freshman class four years ago. You spoke directly to me that morning. In your speech you said that we should set goals, develop plans and work toward achieving our goals."

"Yes, I do recall speaking to your class about those things," I responded.

"Dr. Durley, that is not all you said. You said, 'Don't get discouraged. Don't give up when the going is hard. Keep looking to God and God will see you through.' I have had all those things happen to me – discouragement, doubt and fear of failure, but I recalled what you said and I made it, I made it through."

This encounter, the remembrance of years gone by and his enthusiasm was all happening so fast I had no time to process my feelings. About this time, I noted that twenty-five or thirty graduating seniors had gathered around Steven and me. To be more exact, this group of fellows and I were standing in the shadow of the Howard Thurman statue that is on the Morehouse College campus. Howard Thurman was a great spiritual leader until his death in 1981. He had done much to create racial harmony and hope for a better world. He had served as Dean of Rankin Chapel at Howard University, which was marked in my mind as the place that my spiritual journey began in earnest. One of the things that Dr. Thurman is reported to have said fits with the young men gathered around me and the special moment we were sharing. Dr. Thurman said, "Don't ask yourself what the world needs. Ask yourself what makes you come alive and then go do that. Because the world needs people who have come alive."

As the young men and I were gathered in a *kairos* moment, no greater word could have been spoken to them than those uttered by Howard Thurman some years ago. While this was soaking into all of us, one of the fellows said, "Dr. Durley, will you pray for us?"

Of course I did. I don't recall all that I prayed that morning, but I suggested that we form a circle and all hold hands and thank God for this day. We formed a circle and I lifted my voice to God in thanksgiving for each of the men and what they would be sharing with the world.

I got the tickets that would admit Muriel and me to the Commencement Service, which was being addressed by President Barack Obama. Then, I rushed to my car to get to a luncheon meeting on time. As I got in the car, I realized something special had just happened to me. My heart was beating faster and my mind was quivering with a sense of awe and appreciation. I felt alive, really alive. I felt full of joy and peace.

When I got to the luncheon, I began to talk about the experience with a friend. I had to unpack what had just happened to me. First, it dawned on me that if I had been five minutes earlier or five minutes later, I would not have seen Steven Harris; there would have been no response, no crowd gathering, no celebration and no circling for prayer. Was this God's timing for me? Was it for Steven and the other graduates and not for me? It then occurred to me that speaking to the freshman class four years earlier didn't seem like a major event at the time. I simply did what I was asked to do. Yet, something happened that changed the future of one young man and maybe more. I realized that that simple speech was in reality a seed that brought me an ALIVE moment four years later.

What I had just witnessed demonstrated to me that when you sow good seeds and they are cultivated, the seeds produce an abundant harvest. The harvest in this instance was not the end, but the beginning, the commencement. What can happen in the world because these young men are going out to make a difference? They are alive today and they will have the vision to come alive again and again. What happened to me that day is available not only to me or those fellows with whom I prayed, but to everyone. Are you truly alive right now? Are you excited about your next moment?

When you find that passion, it will give you what the Bible promises, "the peace that passes all understanding." This peace will control how you think, how you feel and how you act. The reason people are dead is because they're not thinking well, not feeling well and, therefore, not behaving well. I'm referring to the walking dead, so to come alive again, they must find their passion. If they do not find their passion, there will be an untreated ache inside. The ache is like the smashed finger I experienced. I had worked hard all day and in the evening I took a steam bath and both my shoulders and my neck were relaxed deeply; my back and my legs were also relaxed and at ease. Then I slammed a door on my finger; the pain in that finger would not go away. The throbbing woke me up deep in the night. Passion is like a throbbing finger. It is searching for something that is meaningful and is filled with peace. It will not stop throbbing until it finds its cure. My back was fine, my hips were fine and everything was good, but that one finger got all the attention. The space in your soul keeps looking for fullness, and it will not quit yearning until it is at peace.

Finally, I stuck that finger into a cup of hot water with sea salt; it felt so good as it relaxed me. My body, mind and spirit started drifting off to sleep as I placed my head on the table; I was so at peace that I did not get back into the bed. The next day I was at a meeting, and a man shook my hand and reminded me with his tight grip that my finger was not well yet. Things happen to remind us that we are not living out our passion. The pain tells us that we need to continue to keep our passion alive. We need to come alive, but we can't come alive with a piece missing. I'm alive when I'm with Muriel; I'm alive when I'm with my children and grandchildren; I'm alive when I feel enlightened and my passion and compassion begin to flow out to others. I'm alive when I imagine that what I'm sharing with you, right now, is having a positive impact on your life, by helping you to come alive.

Life flows through us when we are with others who are alive. If you are a drunk, you can always find someone who wants to drink with you; if you are an addict, you can always find someone who wants to snort coke with you; if you are dead (figuratively speaking), you can always find someone to drive you to the cemetery. To come alive again, you've got to recognize you are in a graveyard situation. Everybody around you is talking graveyard talk. You have to wake up and say, "I want to live again; I want to heal what is broken; I want to find what is missing. I want to recover what is lost. My life has to change. I can feel alive again when my level of expectancy has increased. When I am alive, I know something good is about to transpire in my life. When I look for something good, I usually find it." Dead folks don't expect anything; they're stuck in life just existing from day to day.

Too many people don't believe that they can come alive again. Our friends hang around and expect us to be like we've always been. There are too many doubting Thomases in our lives who will not believe that they cannot come alive again until they thrust a hand into our side and feel that we really are alive. You don't come alive again for others; you come alive for yourself because God is giving you an opportunity to be alive again. When you are alive again, you feel it in your family, in your church, in your relationships, in your aspirations, and in your day-to-day activities. On this side of the resurrection, you can come alive again. Recognize what has been killing you, face what has been hampering your life, and let the light in you shine out.

One of the most amazing and unexpected conversations that I ever had illustrates what I mean by openness, integrity and taking responsibility. Years ago, when I was living in Washington, D.C., the wife of one of the leading bishops in the city came to me for counseling regarding a personal issue of abuse. The bishop was well known throughout the country; he had a radio show and was admired by people in all the churches he oversaw. One day his wife came to my office; she was one of the highly respected first ladies of the city and was at the bishop's right hand wherever he went. I did not know her well because I was not a pastor in their denomination. She had said to one of my friends, "I need to talk with somebody because my life is in shambles and I cannot talk to another preacher in this city. I have no one that I can talk with privately because everyone in the city knows me."

My friend said to her, "I have a friend at Howard Divinity School whose name is Dr. Durley; he majored in psychology; maybe he can be of help." He asked me to talk with her. When she came for the appointment, she seemed so vibrant and alive; she was beautiful and seemingly had everything that money could buy.

We sat down and she began by saying to me, "I'm dead; I don't have any life in me anymore." She stopped and asked, "Can I talk honestly with you? Can I tell you something I've never told anyone?" She emphasized that I had to keep everything she said confidential. Though she was the first lady in the congregation her husband served, she had some things that she needed to get off her heart. She told me that she had two sons; one had finished Princeton and the other had finished Harvard. They were both doing well, and then she stopped speaking, looked me in the eye and said, "The zest has gone out of my life."

I said, "Well, you look vibrant and alive."

She retorted, "But I'm dead on the inside. I'm sixty-four years old and I know I look good on the outside, but that's not the picture on the inside. I am dead on the inside. I have nothing to live for."

I asked, "What killed you?"

She then told me her secret: "For eighteen years, every time the bishop does communion, he gets so deeply involved with his communion service that he comes home and hits me until he sees blood. I've taken his beatings for eighteen years. I feel like a total nobody and as a consequence, I'm dead. Twice I got ready to shoot him, but God held me back. Now, I'm ready to leave him because I can't take it anymore."

I asked, "Do you have anyone to do your eulogy? It is customary for us to bury dead people."

She said, "I'm ready to be buried."

"Are you intending to commit suicide?"

"No, no, no, not suicide. I'm already dead; it's too late to commit suicide. I just can't tolerate the beatings any longer."

After about two and half hours she said, "This is the first time I have talked with anyone about my situation." She indicated that she had passively accepted her husband's abuse, covered for him, and lost her soul in the process. A light began to shine in her as she said, "But now I feel better, cleaner and bright just from having told you why I feel dead. I love that man. I love what he has accomplished. Thank you, thank you so much for listening." Then she began to cry.

"Do you know what I'm going to do? I'm going to tell the bishop just what I've told you. I'm going to confront the bishop; after eighteen years, it's time." As she spoke of her plans, I could see she was beginning the process of beginning to come alive again. I sensed an air of peace, wholeness, direction and joy. She was coming alive. She realized that her Life Was Valuable Everyday. What joy fills us when we come alive again!

We had prayer and she left, and about a year and a half later I saw them on television. She saw me once again at Howard University and she said to me, "Life is so good!"

Both of these persons died years ago, which is the only reason I shared this resurrection story.

Where to Look for Help

The people who can help you come alive are those who have been dead themselves and know what it is to awaken again. They know here and now the power of the resurrection: to lift them out of the grave, out of the cemetery of the living dead and into the light of God's love and power. It's hard for a person who is alive to isolate himself from those who are in darkness. The fulfilled life of a resurrected person must be dedicated to helping others come alive. I think that all of us have been dead at some time in our lives. We have probably even killed a few people with our deadness, which means that we can appreciate even more deeply the light of awakening to a new life.

When you come alive, there is a compulsion to reach out to others to share your life-renewing experience with them – it's the very nature of life, to give itself away. I am sure the people who have been alive know when the energy and the light go out of their souls and the pathway becomes vague and confusing. Yet, people stumbling down the lonely, desolate path have flashbacks, glimpses and glimmers of a different time when life was fuller.

Why Is Resurrection Important to Me?

I'm not sure how to answer this question completely. I'm confident that seeing human life transformed brings me a certain sense of deep fulfillment. I delight in seeing other people come alive. When I was pastoring, I often said to people, "I'll meet you at the hospital." I didn't know whether I wanted them to like me or hoped they would think I was a good man, but in some way it gave me great fulfillment to be with them during their pain and suffering, as well as their joys. Relating to people meaningfully does something for me. I talk to people every day; if I get thirty phone calls, I will answer all of them before I go to sleep. I don't know if there is an ulterior motive in my responses, but I must respond.

When I see someone like Ken come alive or when I see someone like the bishop's wife come alive, I feel like I have experienced a miracle. There's something significant, exciting and rewarding when life once again emerges in someone who had given up on living. When

I say that this work fulfills me, I don't mean narcissistic fulfillment; it is not about me. It is about the other person who was dead and now is alive; it is about churches and communities, and nations coming alive. And this happens incrementally one by one by one. Wow!

Being alive is imperative. To the degree that other people are made alive, I am connected with them in my own aliveness. We all belong together. We are together and there is no escaping it. Paul had it right about the human family: when one suffers, all suffer with him or her. (I Corinthians 12:26) We are in the mix together, and that's why learning to love your neighbor as yourself is also loving yourself through your neighbor.

Will you come alive? And, will you join me in helping others to come alive? Remember,

BE AMAZED

Now I hope you understand why I am AMAZED that my life has been so rich and full when I feel that I haven't deserved it. I'm amazed that my personal lifetime reflections have nurtured me and that there is the possibility that you too may become AMAZED at what God has done and is doing in your life. Aren't you AMAZED that at this precise moment you can come alive again, because *"A LIFE IS VALUABLE EVERYDAY."* Go and live yours!